CW00521980

JOE GILBERT

Titans Of Business

Copyright © 2023 by Joe Gilbert

All rights reserved. No part of this publication may be reproduced, stored or transmitted in any form or by any means, electronic, mechanical, photocopying, recording, scanning, or otherwise without written permission from the publisher. It is illegal to copy this book, post it to a website, or distribute it by any other means without permission.

First edition

This book was professionally typeset on Reedsy.
Find out more at reedsy.com

Contents

1

Forward

When I first embarked on my entrepreneurial journey 8 years ago, the path ahead was not just uncharted but also daunting. Each decision point, from conceptualizing the first product to making that first hire, felt like a litmus test of my acumen. It was during these trying times that I found solace, guidance, and inspiration in the wisdom imparted by business pioneers through their books. Each tome provided a unique perspective, a different piece of the puzzle, helping me navigate the challenges of the business world.

Yet, as the list of recommended reads grew, a new challenge emerged: Time. The hours in a day seemed insufficient to sift through the mounting stack of business books, each promising ground-breaking insights. The realization dawned upon me that while every book had its unique value, there were often overlapping themes, core principles, and shared wisdom. What if there was a concise guide, a compass of sorts, that distilled the essence of these business classics?

This book, dear reader, is the fruit of that idea. Born out of countless hours of reading, reflecting, and implementing, it seeks to present the key takeaways from fifty of the most influential business books of our time. But make no mistake—this is not a replacement for the in-depth wisdom, detailed anecdotes, and vast knowledge that each of these books offers. Instead, think of it as a primer, a starting point, or even a refresher for those who have already delved into these classics.

The aim is simple: to offer high-level insights and summaries, shedding light on the core learnings that have shaped the trajectory of countless successful entrepreneurs, leaders, and innovators. Whether you're just starting out or are a seasoned professional, there's something in here for everyone.

As you flip through the pages, you'll uncover distilled wisdom from giants in the industry, lessons hard-won from the trenches of the business battlefield, and strategies that have stood the test of time. Dive in, draw from this wellspring of knowledge, and may the insights contained herein illuminate your path, just as the original books did for me.

Welcome to the pantheon of business wisdom. Let's embark on this enlightening journey together.

2

"Good to Great" by Jim Collins

In "Good to Great," Jim Collins seeks to answer a fundamental business question: Why do some companies make the leap from good to outstanding performance and sustain it, while others do not? Through rigorous research, Collins and his team identified a set of common characteristics among companies that underwent this transformation. These characteristics can be encapsulated in several core concepts:

Level 5 Leadership:

- **Definition:** Leaders who combine personal humility with professional will.
- **Impact:** These leaders prioritize the organization's success over their ego. They're often not "celebrity" CEOs but work diligently behind the scenes.
- **Legacy:** Level 5 leaders set up their successors for success, contrasting with less effective leaders who might set their successors up for failure.

First Who, Then What:

- **Concept:** Before determining the direction a company should take, it's crucial to get the right people on board (and the wrong ones off).
- **Importance:** Having a committed, competent team means that when the company does find the right direction, it can move more effectively.

The Hedgehog Concept:

- **Origin:** Derived from the parable of the fox (who knows many things) and the hedgehog (who knows one big thing).
- **Implementation:** Companies should focus on what they can be the best at, what drives their economic engine, and what they're passionate about.
- **Relevance:** It's about simplicity and clarity. Companies shouldn't stretch themselves thin over various domains but rather focus on their core competency.

The Flywheel and the Doom Loop:

- **Flywheel Effect:** Good-to-great transformations don't happen overnight. They result from persistent pushing in a consistent direction over time.
- **Doom Loop:** In contrast, companies that jump from one new direction or trend to another without any consistency don't achieve the sustained results of the flywheel effect.

Culture of Discipline:

- **Significance:** A blend of discipline in people, thought, and action can ensure sustained greatness.
- **Operational Efficiency:** With disciplined people, there's no need for hierarchy; with disciplined thought, there's no need for bureaucracy; with disciplined action, there's no need for excessive controls.

Technology Accelerators:

- **Observation:** Good-to-great companies don't necessarily focus on technology for technology's sake.
- **Application:** Technology is seen as an accelerator of momentum, not a creator of it. It's applied in alignment with the Hedgehog Concept.

The Stockdale Paradox:

- **Concept:** Named after Admiral Jim Stockdale, it's the idea of confronting the brutal facts of one's current reality while maintaining unwavering faith that they'll prevail in the end.
- **Significance:** It underscores the importance of honesty and realism paired with a long-term optimism.

Why "Good to Great" Is Critically Acclaimed:

Jim Collins' "Good to Great" offers a data-driven examination of corporate success, breaking away from quick fixes and buzzword-driven strategies. Its empirical nature and the timelessness of its principles have made it a mainstay in business literature. The book underscores the fact that greatness is not a function of circumstance; it's a matter of conscious choice and discipline. Whether for organizational leaders, managers, or individual contributors, the insights from "Good to Great" are transformative, fostering long-term, sustainable excellence over mere temporal success.

3

"The Innovator's Dilemma" by Clayton M. Christensen

"The Innovator's Dilemma," penned by Harvard Business School professor Clayton M. Christensen, is a seminal work that explores the complex reasons successful companies can lose their market leadership, especially due to new, innovative entrants in the market. Christensen brings a fresh perspective on why certain business practices, which are considered best practices in mainstream contexts, might cripple giants when it comes to disruptive innovations.

Understanding Disruption:

- **Sustaining vs. Disruptive:** Christensen differentiates between sustaining innovations (those that improve current products) and disruptive innovations (those that, initially, might not be as good as current products but are cheaper or serve different needs, thus creating new markets).
- **Initial Market Reaction:** Disruptive innovations often target overlooked segments, and because they don't address

mainstream markets initially, established companies may disregard them.

Value Networks:

- **Definition:** The context within which a firm identifies customer needs, acquires resources, and competes.
- **Role in Dilemma:** Once a company establishes a value network, it prioritizes innovations that help it sustain and enhance its position in that network. This focus can make the company blind to disruptive innovations that do not fit within its existing value network.

Resource Dependence:

- **Company DNA:** Companies get proficient in what they repeatedly do, creating a DNA of sorts. Over time, this DNA becomes rigid and can be a barrier to adopting new innovations.
- **Resource Allocation:** Established companies allocate resources to the most profitable segments, often sidelining disruptive innovations that promise lesser immediate returns.

The Dilemma for Incumbents:

- **Pursuing Profit:** Established companies often avoid investing in disruptive technologies because, initially, they are not as profitable and may even jeopardize existing relationships with customers and profit structures.
- **Missed Opportunities:** By the time the bigger players

realize the potential of the disruptive innovation, newer entrants have often established themselves.

Organizational Inertia:

- **Impact:** Well-established companies have set processes, values, and a defined culture. These factors can lead to inertia, making it difficult for these companies to respond to disruptive forces swiftly.
- **Overcoming Inertia:** Christensen suggests that established firms, to tackle disruptive innovations, might need to set up separate teams or units that operate outside the firm's usual value network and can adopt a startup's agility.

Solutions to the Dilemma:

- **Small Markets Don't Solve Big Company Needs:** Recognizing that disruptive technologies initially cater to smaller markets can help big firms strategize effectively.
- **Separate Organizations:** Creating an autonomous organization that can thrive in emerging disruptive sectors can help harness the power of disruption without affecting the parent organization's mainstream operations.

Why "The Innovator's Dilemma" Is Profoundly Influential:

Clayton M. Christensen's "The Innovator's Dilemma" has been a touchstone in business literature since its publication. The book's insights are counter-intuitive; it paints a picture where doing everything "right" in conventional business wisdom can still lead to failure in the face of disruption. Christensen's framework has provided leaders, managers, and entrepreneurs with invaluable perspectives on innovation, competition, and organizational dynamics. The book's influence extends beyond the business realm, resonating with thinkers and practitioners in various sectors who grapple with the challenges and opportunities presented by disruptive change.

4

"How to Win Friends and Influence People" by Dale Carnegie

Published in 1936, Dale Carnegie's classic self-help book, "How to Win Friends and Influence People," remains a bestseller, and its principles have endured through decades because of their universal applicability. The book offers practical and straightforward advice to help individuals navigate social situations, win others over, and become more persuasive in interactions.

Fundamental Techniques in Handling People:

- **Avoid Criticism and Complaint:** Carnegie argues that criticism is futile because it puts people on the defensive and usually makes them strive to justify themselves. It's more effective to encourage and compliment.
- **Give Honest and Sincere Appreciation:** Genuine appreciation, not flattery, is essential. Everyone wants a feeling of importance; acknowledgment satisfies this fundamental need in individuals.
- **Arouse an Eager Want:** Always frame interactions in terms

of what the other person wants. By understanding and considering their desires, you can motivate them to see things from your perspective.

Ways to Make People Like You:

- **Genuine Interest:** Taking genuine interest in others is the best way to win friends. It's a simple act that makes a significant difference.
- **Smile:** A smile says, "I like you. You make me happy."
- **Remember Names:** Carnegie mentions that a person's name is the sweetest sound to them. Remembering names and using them in conversations makes interactions personal and sincere.
- **Be a Good Listener:** Allowing others to talk, and actively listening to them, makes them feel valued.
- **Discuss What Matters to Them:** Dive into subjects that the other person cherishes.
- **Make Them Feel Important:** Recognize their importance sincerely, without being manipulative or flattering.

Win People to Your Way of Thinking:

- **Avoid Arguments:** They cannot be won. Even if you win, you lose goodwill.
- **Show Respect for Opinions:** You can't change someone's mind by telling them they are wrong.
- **Admit Mistakes:** Admitting one's errors clears the air of defensiveness.
- **Begin in a Friendly Way:** It sets the tone for constructive

dialogue.
- **Let the Person Say "Yes":** Start conversations in areas of agreement.
- **Let Them Feel the Idea is Theirs:** This makes them more invested in the idea.
- **Understand Their Perspective:** By genuinely trying to understand another's viewpoint, you open doors to more significant influence.

Change People Without Offense:

- **Indirectly Point Out Mistakes:** This method is less confrontational and more effective.
- **Give Them a Reputation to Live Up To:** If you want someone to improve in a particular area, act as though they already have that trait or skill.
- **Encourage and Make Faults Seem Easy to Correct:** Encouragement boosts confidence, making the journey of change seem attainable.
- **Make Them Happy to Do What You Propose:** Motivation often comes from personal happiness or satisfaction.

Why "How to Win Friends and Influence People" Is Timelessly Relevant:

Dale Carnegie's book is not just about succeeding in the business world; it's a guide to human relations. Its principles are grounded in understanding human nature and the deep-seated desires that drive people: the hunger for genuine appreciation, the longing to feel important, and the need to be understood.

The book is a treasure trove of actionable insights that resonate because they're based on the simple act of showing genuine interest and respect towards others. In an age where communication is more vital than ever, Carnegie's teachings offer timeless wisdom on building authentic, meaningful connections with those around us.

5

"The Lean Startup" by Eric Ries

"The Lean Startup" is a groundbreaking book that presents a systematic, scientific approach for creating and managing successful startups in the contemporary business landscape, characterized by unprecedented uncertainty and rapid change. The methodology is rooted in the principles of lean manufacturing, adapted for the context of startups.

Minimum Viable Product (MVP):

- Concept: Start with the simplest form of your idea to expedite the learning process.
- Importance: The MVP helps entrepreneurs begin the process of learning as quickly as possible. It's not necessarily about the product being perfect or even complete; it's about testing assumptions and hypotheses.
- Examples: Dropbox started with a simple video demonstrating its technology, and Groupon began as a WordPress site.

Build-Measure-Learn Loop:

- Concept: Convert ideas into products, gauge how customers respond, then learn to either pivot or persevere.
- Importance: This feedback loop emphasizes the need for rapid iterations to test assumptions and get closer to product-market fit.
- Practice: If a startup's hypothesis is proven wrong, it's better to find out quickly rather than after investing a lot of time and resources.

Validated Learning:

- Concept: The goal of startups is to learn what customers genuinely want. This learning can be scientifically validated.
- Importance: Focus on real-world validations rather than just relying on theoretical assumptions or intuitions. Metrics, analytics, and experiments serve this purpose.
- Example: Running A/B tests on website features to determine which one resonates more with users.

Continuous Deployment:

- Concept: Implement a consistent and fast cycle of releasing products to acquire immediate feedback.
- Importance: Quick iterations can help fix mistakes and cater to customer needs swiftly.
- Practice: Some companies deploy new code into production multiple times a day to stay agile and responsive.

Metrics – Actionable vs. Vanity:

- Concept: Not all metrics are equally useful. Some might look good on paper but don't provide insights that lead to actionable changes.
- Importance: Vanity metrics might boost ego but don't help in long-term growth. Actionable metrics provide a clearer path to sustainable growth.
- Example: While a website might boast high page views (vanity metric), the conversion rate (actionable metric) could be more important for business growth.

Sustainability:

- Concept: Adapt and adjust the business model based on real feedback before committing large resources.
- Importance: This prevents startups from heading down the wrong path for too long and ensures resources are utilized most effectively.

Pivot or Persevere:

- Concept: Once feedback from the MVP is gathered, startups face a crucial decision.
- Importance: The data will reveal whether the current course is sustainable or if there's a need to make a structural course correction.
- Example: Slack started as a gaming company but pivoted to become a communication platform after gauging the real need in the market.

Why "The Lean Startup" Stands Out:

Eric Ries's "The Lean Startup" offers a revolutionary approach to business endeavors, challenging traditional norms of product development and business strategy. While traditional models advocate for robust planning and prediction, Ries emphasizes adaptability, rapid feedback, and iterative design. In a business climate where change is the only constant, this methodology resonates profoundly. From solopreneurs to large corporations, the principles of "The Lean Startup" have found widespread application, making it an invaluable resource for anyone aiming to innovate and succeed in today's dynamic market landscape.

6

"The E-Myth Revisited" by Michael E. Gerber

Michael E. Gerber's "The E-Myth Revisited: Why Most Small Businesses Don't Work and What to Do About It" delves into the myths surrounding entrepreneurship and offers a structured approach for small business owners to thrive, not just survive. The book argues that knowing the technical side of a business doesn't necessarily mean one can successfully run a business in that field.

The E-Myth:

- **Definition:** The Entrepreneurial Myth, which is the mistaken belief that most businesses are started by entrepreneurs risking capital to make a profit. In reality, most are started by technicians (e.g., bakers, plumbers) who know the technical work but not necessarily how to run such a business.
- **Consequences:** The technician's mindset can become a limitation, leading to a business that heavily relies on its

owner and struggles to scale or even operate efficiently.

Three Personalities of a Business Owner:

- **Entrepreneur:** The dreamer, visionary, and innovator.
- **Manager:** The planner, who thrives on order and predictability.
- **Technician:** The doer, who loves the technical work at hand.
- **Balancing Act:** Successful business owners must strike a balance between these roles, ensuring the business has vision, order, and technical competence.

Infancy, Adolescence, and Maturity in Business:

- **Infancy:** The technician's phase, where the owner is involved in every aspect of the business.
- **Adolescence:** Growth phase, where the owner might consider getting help. The business faces growing pains as delegation begins.
- **Maturity:** The entrepreneurial perspective emerges, marking the phase where the business has a clear vision and consistent operating procedures.

The Franchise Prototype:

- **Concept:** Gerber advocates for creating systems and processes in the business as if it were going to be replicated 5,000 times, much like a franchise.
- **Advantages:** This approach ensures consistency, predictability, and scalability. It allows the business to work

independently of the owner.

Working On Your Business, Not In It:

- **Distinction:** Business owners should shift from doing daily technical tasks (working in the business) to designing, building, and refining the system (working on the business).
- **Significance:** This shift enables businesses to grow, scale, and eventually function independently of the owner's constant involvement.

The Business Development Process:

- **Innovation:** Continual improvement and adaptation based on customer feedback and industry changes.
- **Quantification:** Tracking and measuring all aspects of the business for informed decision-making.
- **Orchestration:** Ensuring consistent delivery by standardizing and systematizing processes.

Why "The E-Myth Revisited" Is Pivotal for Small Business Owners:

Michael E. Gerber's book has resonated with many business owners because it addresses a critical challenge: the conflict between the role of the technician and that of the business owner. By introducing systems and processes and shifting from working in the business to working on it, owners can create entities that can thrive without their constant intervention.

The principles in "The E-Myth Revisited" offer a blueprint for transforming small businesses from chaotic, owner-reliant operations into organized, scalable enterprises. It's a guide to freedom from the daily grind and a roadmap to creating businesses that can achieve both profitability and longevity.

7

"Influence: The Psychology of Persuasion" by Robert B. Cialdini

Robert B. Cialdini's "Influence" is a seminal work on the art and science of persuasion. Through extensive research, Cialdini identifies six fundamental principles or "weapons of influence" that can lead people to say "yes" without thinking critically. These principles are tools that skilled persuaders—ranging from salespeople to politicians—use, sometimes manipulatively, to convince others.

Reciprocity:

- **Definition:** The social obligation to repay what another person has given to us.
- **Examples:** If someone invites us to a party, we feel compelled to invite them to ours. In sales, free samples can trigger a sense of indebtedness.
- **Exploitation:** Manipulative individuals can use this by doing unsolicited favors and then expecting something much larger in return.

Commitment and Consistency:

- **Definition:** Once a choice is made, individuals feel internal and external pressure to behave consistently with that commitment.
- **Examples:** Asking someone to sign a public petition increases the chance they'll later donate to the cause.
- **Exploitation:** The "foot-in-the-door" technique, where agreeing to a small initial request increases the likelihood of agreeing to a subsequent larger request.

Social Proof:

- **Definition:** Individuals look to others to determine what is correct behavior, especially in uncertain situations.
- **Examples:** Laugh tracks on TV shows or bars using 'plants' to look busier than they are.
- **Exploitation:** Displaying testimonials or creating fake social buzz around products.

Authority:

- **Definition:** People have a deep-seated sense of duty to authority.
- **Examples:** Titles, uniforms, and luxury cars lend an air of prestige and credibility.
- **Exploitation:** Fake professionals endorsing products, or using actors in doctor's attire for commercials.

Liking:

- **Definition:** People are more inclined to be influenced by people they like.
- **Factors Contributing to Liking:** Physical attractiveness, similarity, compliments, cooperative endeavors, and associative conditioning.
- **Exploitation:** Salespeople using flattery or mimicking customer behavior to establish rapport.

Scarcity:

- **Definition:** Opportunities seem more valuable when they are less available.
- **Examples:** Limited-time offers or flash sales create a sense of urgency.
- **Exploitation:** Artificially creating a sense of scarcity to accelerate decisions.

Why "Influence: The Psychology of Persuasion" Is a Must-Read:

Robert B. Cialdini's "Influence" isn't just a book about the tactics used in sales or marketing; it's a deep dive into the human psyche and our inherent vulnerabilities in decision-making. It holds a mirror up to everyday situations, making readers aware of how they can be influenced, often without realizing it. For those in professions that rely on persuasion, it offers invaluable insights. For the general reader, it's a guide to navigating a world full of subtle and not-so-subtle persuasions, arming them with awareness and understanding. By unraveling the mechanics of influence, Cialdini empowers readers to make more informed choices and resist manipulative tactics.

8

"The 7 Habits of Highly Effective People" by Stephen R. Covey

Stephen R. Covey's "The 7 Habits of Highly Effective People" has left an indelible mark on the self-help genre. Covey introduces a principle-centered approach for addressing both personal and interpersonal challenges. The habits are organized in a sequence, taking one from dependence to independence and finally to interdependence.

Be Proactive (Personal Responsibility):

- **Definition:** Take control of your own actions and behaviors. Recognize the freedom to choose your response to stimuli.
- **Core Idea:** We are in control of our own actions and attitudes. It's essential to focus on what we can change—the circle of influence—rather than what we can't—the circle of concern.

Begin with the End in Mind (Vision):

- **Definition:** Clearly define what you want to achieve in the long run.
- **Core Idea:** Envision your own funeral. How do you want to be remembered? By determining your ultimate end, you can work backward and design a life aligned with these deeper values and goals.

Put First Things First (Prioritization):

- **Definition:** Prioritize your time and tasks based on importance, not urgency.
- **Core Idea:** Spend time in "Quadrant II," which includes tasks that are important but not urgent. This quadrant emphasizes proactive behavior, such as building relationships and planning.

Think Win-Win (Mutual Benefit):

- **Definition:** Adopt an abundance mentality, where you seek mutual benefits in interpersonal interactions.
- **Core Idea:** Effective, long-term relationships are built on mutual respect and mutual benefit, not competition.

Seek First to Understand, Then to Be Understood (Empathetic Communication):

- **Definition:** Before offering advice or solutions, deeply understand the other person's perspective.
- **Core Idea:** True empathetic listening builds trust and opens the door for more meaningful communication and problem-solving.

Synergize (Collaborative Teamwork):

- **Definition:** Achieve goals through cooperative efforts, leveraging the strengths of a team.
- **Core Idea:** The whole is greater than the sum of its parts. Collaborative efforts can yield results that individuals alone couldn't achieve.

Sharpen the Saw (Self-Renewal):

- **Definition:** Regularly renew and strengthen each of the four dimensions of your nature: physical, mental, emotional/social, and spiritual.
- **Core Idea:** Continuous self-growth and self-care ensure sustainability and longevity in all endeavors.

Why "The 7 Habits of Highly Effective People" Is a Transformational Book:

Stephen R. Covey's book isn't just about habits; it's about shifting one's worldview and adopting a principle-centered paradigm. Instead of looking for quick fixes, Covey focuses on enduring principles that have stood the test of time. These habits are not just to-do lists; they require deep internalization and practice. By addressing both personal and interpersonal effectiveness, Covey offers a holistic framework for life mastery, making this book a timeless resource for anyone seeking to lead a life of significance and purpose.

9

"Zero to One" by Peter Thiel

"Zero to One" offers an unconventional perspective on innovation and startup culture. Written by Peter Thiel, a cofounder of PayPal and a prominent venture capitalist, the book challenges popular beliefs about business and provides insights into creating truly unique companies.

Zero to One vs. One to N:

- **Definition:** Going from "zero to one" means creating something entirely new, whereas going from "one to n" signifies iterating on what already exists.
- **Core Idea:** True innovation doesn't come from copying what's already successful but from pioneering entirely new avenues.

Monopolies:

- **Definition:** Companies that are so good at what they do that they face no direct competition.

- **Core Idea:** Strive to build monopolies. They are profitable, allow for long-term planning, and are more capable of doing good for society than competition-driven entities.

Power Law Dynamics:

- **Definition:** In a venture portfolio, a single stellar company can outperform all others combined.
- **Core Idea:** Investors and entrepreneurs should seek and invest in ventures that have the potential to become that one outsized success.

Last Mover Advantage:

- **Definition:** The value of being the last mover in a market, solidifying a monopoly position.
- **Core Idea:** It's not always about being first; it's about capturing the market sustainably. Think of Google, which wasn't the first search engine but is now the dominant player.

Foundations:

- **Definition:** The beginning of a startup, which determines its trajectory.
- **Core Idea:** The early decisions, from co-founders to company culture, can make or break the future of a company.

Secrets:

- **Definition:** Truths not widely recognized or believed,

which can be the foundation for a successful company.

- **Core Idea:** Entrepreneurs should seek out secrets about the world — unexplored territories that can lead to innovation.

The Mechanics of Mafia:

- **Definition:** The tight-knit culture and camaraderie found in successful startups.
- **Core Idea:** Building a close-knit team, like the "PayPal Mafia," ensures commitment, trust, and aligned ambition.

Escaping the Flat World:

- **Definition:** A challenge to globalized sameness, emphasizing unique approaches.
- **Core Idea:** Instead of following the crowd, businesses should focus on singular challenges and unique solutions.

Why "Zero to One" Is a Must-Read for Aspiring Entrepreneurs:

Peter Thiel's "Zero to One" is more than a business book—it's a philosophical take on startups and innovation. Thiel challenges conventional wisdom, such as the value of competition, and provides counterintuitive insights, emphasizing the significance of building something unique rather than iterating on existing ideas. He combines his vast experience with thoughtful commentary, making this book a treasure trove of unconventional wisdom. For entrepreneurs looking to make a meaningful impact and build the next "unicorn," "Zero to

One" offers a roadmap that diverges from the usual paths and ventures into uncharted territories.

10

"The Hard Thing About Hard Things" by Ben Horowitz

Ben Horowitz, co-founder of the venture capital firm Andreessen Horowitz, offers insights gleaned from his own experiences as a startup founder, CEO, and venture capitalist in "The Hard Thing About Hard Things." The book is a candid reflection on the difficult challenges and dark moments entrepreneurs face but are seldom discussed openly.

No Easy Answers:

- **Definition:** Unlike most business problems, the hard problems have no proven formula for resolution.
- **Core Idea:** The most challenging aspects of running a company don't have recipes for success. They require judgment calls in tough situations.

War and Peace:

- **Definition:** The contrasting phases of business—growth

and battles for market share versus consolidation and defending position.

· **Core Idea:** The strategies required in the "war" phase differ from those in the "peace" phase. Leaders must be adaptable.

Struggle is Part of the Journey:

· **Definition:** The internal battle and existential crisis a founder or CEO often faces.
· **Core Idea:** Building a company is inherently tough, and the struggle is natural. Leaders often feel despair, but pushing through is crucial.

Taking Care of People:

· **Definition:** The responsibility of leaders to ensure the welfare of their team.
· **Core Idea:** Managing layoffs, maintaining morale, and ensuring a positive company culture even in tough times is crucial.

Embrace the Hard Decisions:

· **Definition:** The necessity to make and act upon difficult choices.
· **Core Idea:** Whether it's firing a loyal but underperforming employee, or pivoting a product, CEOs need to make hard decisions for the company's greater good.

Telling It Like It Is:

- **Definition:** The value of transparency and honesty in communication.
- **Core Idea:** Whether delivering bad news or discussing failures, straightforwardness is essential for trust and clarity.

Learning on the Job:

- **Definition:** The continuous journey of learning and adapting.
- **Core Idea:** Being a CEO is one of the few jobs that nobody is truly trained for. Leaders learn through experience, mentorship, and continuous reflection.

Why "The Hard Thing About Hard Things" Is a Compelling Read for Entrepreneurs:

Ben Horowitz's "The Hard Thing About Hard Things" stands out in the business book genre because of its raw, unfiltered look at the tribulations of entrepreneurship. It isn't a guide about the rosy path to success; it's about navigating the thorns along the way. Horowitz provides firsthand anecdotes from his experiences, adding weight to his advice. For entrepreneurs, this book is both a comfort and a guide—it acknowledges the inherent difficulties in their journey while providing insights to navigate them. Rather than offering idealistic advice, Horowitz provides wisdom drawn from the trenches, making this book a touchstone for startup leaders navigating the tumultuous waters of business.

11

"Blue Ocean Strategy" by W. Chan Kim & Renée Mauborgne

"Blue Ocean Strategy" challenges the traditional business approach focused on competition and offers an innovative framework for value creation. The authors, W. Chan Kim and Renée Mauborgne, contend that lasting success doesn't come from battling competitors but from creating blue oceans of uncontested market space.

Red Oceans vs. Blue O...

- **Definition:** The simultaneous pursuit of differentiation and low cost.
- **Core Idea:** Companies can break the trade-off between differentiation and cost by innovating in a manner that adds value for both the company and its customers.

Strategy Canvas:

- **Definition:** A diagnostic tool to represent an organization's strategic profile in terms of factors it competes on.
- **Core Idea:** By plotting current and desired strategies on the canvas, businesses can visualize areas for differentiation and innovation.

Four Actions Framework:

- **Definition:** A tool to reconstruct market boundaries.
- **Core Idea:** By questioning the strategic logic of industry practices, companies can:

1. **Eliminate** factors the industry has taken for granted.
2. **Reduce** factors below the industry standard.
3. **Raise** factors above the industry standard.
4. **Create** new factors the industry has never offered.
5. **Six Paths Framework:**

- **Definition:** A guide to explore untapped market space.
- **Core Idea:** Companies can look across:

1. Alternative industries.
2. Strategic groups.

3. The chain of buyers.
4. Complementary product and service offerings.
5. Functional or emotional appeal.
6. Time.

Overcome Key Organizational Hurdles:

- **Definition:** Techniques to overcome the cognitive, resource, motivational, and political hurdles in executing a blue ocean strategy.
- **Core Idea:** Innovative strategy requires innovative execution.

Build Execution into Strategy:

- **Definition:** Ensuring that strategy formulation and execution are intertwined.
- **Core Idea:** People committed to the strategy are crucial for its successful execution. By involving them in the strategy-making process, you gain their buy-in from the outset.

The book's unique approach encourages businesses to think beyond conventional strategies and opens a world of creativity and innovation. For leaders and strategists, it provides a visionary roadmap for sustainable growth and success in any industry.

12

"6 Months to 6 Figures" by Peter Voogd

In "6 Months to 6 Figures," Peter Voogd, a serial entrepreneur and business coach, lays out a roadmap for young entrepreneurs to achieve financial success in a short span of time. Drawing from his personal experiences, Voogd details the steps, mindset shifts, and strategies that propelled him from a place of struggle to achieving six figures in just six months.

Absolute Clarity:

- **Core Idea:** Letting go of an employee mindset and taking charge as an entrepreneur means you focus on results, not just effort.

High-Value Activities:

- **Definition:** Tasks that bring the most significant results or move you closest to your goals.
- **Core Idea:** Time should be dedicated to high-impact tasks. Prioritize activities that align directly with your financial and business goals.

Mastery vs. Overload:

- **Definition:** Focusing on mastering essential skills rather than trying to juggle too many tasks.
- **Core Idea:** Instead of being overwhelmed with information, concentrate on mastering key skills crucial for your business's success.

Influence and Association:

- **Definition:** Surrounding oneself with people who uplift, inspire, and challenge you.
- **Core Idea:** Your network greatly influences your net worth. Surrounding yourself with successful and positive individuals can accelerate your journey.

Consistent Energy and Motivation:

- **Definition:** Keeping up the momentum and staying moti-

vated throughout the journey.
- **Core Idea:** Consistency is key. Ensuring you're physically, mentally, and emotionally tuned can help you maintain high levels of productivity.

Results-Focused Routine:

- **Definition:** Building habits and routines that are geared towards results.
- **Core Idea:** Establishing daily, weekly, and monthly routines that prioritize goal-centric activities ensures steady progress towards six figures.

Why "6 Months to 6 Figures" Is a Valuable Guide for Aspiring Entrepreneurs:

Peter Voogd's "6 Months to 6 Figures" is a reflection of his personal journey sprinkled with actionable insights for others to follow. Rather than abstract concepts, Voogd focuses on practical steps and strategies, making the book a hand-

13

"The Five Dysfunctions of a Team" by Patrick Lencioni

In "The Five Dysfunctions of a Team," Patrick Lencioni identifies common problems that teams face, illustrating them through a fable about a fictional firm's executive team. He then provides actionable insights and strategies to overcome these dysfunctions. The five dysfunctions he discusses, in the order they are presented, are:

Absence of Trust:

- **Definition:** The fear of vulnerability among team members, which prevents them from being open about mistakes, weaknesses, or needs for help
- **Core Idea:** Trust is the foundation of any cohesive team. Teams can overcome this dysfunction by fostering vulnerability-based trust where members are comfortable being open and honest with one another.

Fear of Conflict:

- **Definition:** Teams that lack trust are incapable of engaging in passionate, unfiltered debate about key issues, causing harmful conflicts to go unresolved.
- **Core Idea:** Constructive conflicts are essential for making sound decisions. Teams should encourage open discussions and disagreements on ideas and decisions.

Lack of Commitment:

- **Definition:** Without conflict, it's difficult for team members to commit to decisions, leading to ambiguity among the team about direction and priorities.
- **Core Idea:** By ensuring that all opinions and ideas are debated, teams can confidently commit to a clear plan of action.

Avoidance of Accountability:

- **Definition:** Teams that don't commit to a clear plan of action hesitate to call their peers on actions and behaviors that may seem counterproductive to the overall good of the lective results over individual recognition or other personal interests.

Why "The Five Dysfunctions of a Team" Is a Must-Read for Team Leaders and Members:

Patrick Lencioni's "The Five Dysfunctions of a Team" offers a unique combination of storytelling and actionable advice, making it both engaging and practical. By presenting the dysfunctions in a fable format, Lencioni humanizes the challenges, making them relatable to a wide range of readers. The clear structure and hierarchy of the dysfunctions provide a diagnostic tool for teams to assess their shortcomings and strategies to address them. Whether you're a leader aiming to create a cohesive team or a team member looking to contribute more effectively, this book provides invaluable insights into the dynamics of team interaction and collaboration.

14

"Start with Why" by Simon Sinek

"Start with Why" presents the idea that successful individuals and organizations are those that have a clear understanding of their "Why" – their purpose, cause, or belief that drives them. Simon Sinek posits that understanding this "Why" is what allows these entities to inspire others and achieve remarkable things.

The Golden Circle:

- **Definition:** "Why" is not a profit. It's a purpose, cause, or belief.
- **Core Idea:** While making money is essential for the vitality and sustainability of a business, it's not the reason a business exists. Money is a result.

The Biology of the Golden Circle:

- **Definition:** The Golden Circle aligns with the three major levels of the brain, corresponding to the decision-making process.
- **Core Idea:** The limbic brain, which is responsible for feelings like trust and loyalty, aligns with the "Why." It's where decision-making happens. This is why appealing to people's emotions (i.e., their "Why") is so effective.

Manipulation vs. Inspiration:

- **Definition:** Manipulations (e.g., price reductions, promotions) are ways to generate a transaction or behavior without building loyalty. Inspiration is the ability to mobilize people towards a shared vision.
- **Core Idea:** While manipulations can drive short-term results, they don't foster loyalty or a lasting connection. Starting with "Why" leads to inspiration and long-term loyalty.

The Diffusion of Innovations:

- **Definition:** An idea conceptualized by Everett Rogers that classifies people into categories based on their adoption of

innovations: Innovators, Early Adopters, Early Majority, Late Majority, and Laggards.
- **Core Idea:** Those who start with "Why" are able to attract the early adopters and achieve market success that then cascades to broader populations.

Clarity, Discipline, and Consistency:

- **Definition:** The three things needed to harness the power of "Why."
- **Core Idea:** Leaders and organizations must be clear about their "Why," be disciplined in how they bring it to life, and be consistent in what they do and say.

Why "Start with Why" is a Thought-Provoking Guide for Leaders:

Simon Sinek's "Start with Why" is a rallying cry for those aiming to inspire others and create lasting change. By diving into the core essence of inspiration and its ...

15

"The Art of Strategy" by Avinash K. Dixit & Barry J. Nalebuff

"The Art of Strategy" is a comprehensive guide to the world of game theory, breaking down complex concepts into relatable examples and scenarios. Game theory, at its core, studies strategic interactions among rational players. Dixit and Nalebuff provide a deep dive into how individuals and organizations can leverage this powerful tool in various decision-making contexts.

Basics of Game Theory:

- **Definition:** Game theory is the study of mathematical models of strategic interactions among rational decision-makers.
- **Core Idea:** Every strategic situation involves players, actions, and payoffs. By understanding the dynamics of these elements, individuals can anticipate the moves of others and respond strategically

Sequential Games:

- **Definition:** Games where players move in sequence, often visualized using a game tree.
- **Core Idea:** In these games, the key is to think forward and reason backward. Anticipate what you'd do in future situations, then determine what you should do in the present.

Simultaneous Games:

- **Definition:** Games where players move at the same time.
- **Core Idea:** Since players choose their actions without knowing the choice of the opponent, they should focus on strategies that work best given what the opponent might do.

Strategy and Commitment:

- **Definition:** The act of making a binding decision that influences an opponent's behavior

Cooperation and Coordination:

- **Definition:** Scenarios where players can benefit from cooperating or coordinating their actions.
- **Core Idea:** Even in competitive situations, there can be opportunities for mutual benefit if players can find ways to trust and collaborate.

Mechanism Design:

- **Definition:** Instead of taking a game as given and then finding the best strategy, it's about designing the game itself to achieve a desired outcome.
- **Core Idea:** By shaping the rules of the game, one can guide players toward a specific outcome.

Applications in Real Life:

- **Definition:** Using game theory to analyze various real-world scenarios, from auctions to political campaigns.
- **Core Idea:** Game theory isn't just a theoretical framework; it has practical implications in diverse areas like business, politics, and everyday decision-making.

Why "The Art of Strategy" is a Must-Read for Strategic Thinkers:

Dixit and Nalebuff, through "The Art of Strategy," transform the often abstract and mathematical world of game theory into something tangible and deeply relevant. The book's strength lies in its ability to draw connections between theoretical concepts and real-world situations, making it accessible to both novices and experts. For anyone aiming to sharpen their strategic thinking, whether in business, politics, or daily life, this book offers a masterclass in understanding and navigating complex interactions.

16

"Drive: The Surprising Truth About What Motivates Us" by Daniel H. Pink

"Drive" delves into human motivation, challenging traditional beliefs and presenting a new framework. Daniel Pink argues that while the old model of motivation (carrots and sticks, or rewards and punishments) worked in the 20th century, it's inadequate for today's challenges. Instead, he introduces a more nuanced, intrinsic model centered on autonomy, mastery, and purpose.

The Three Elements of Motivation:

- **Autonomy:** The desire to direct our own lives. Pink suggests that allowing employees to have autonomy over some or all of the four T's (Task, Time, Technique, and Team) can lead to higher levels of creativity and productivity.
- **Mastery:** The urge to become better at something that matters. This isn't about reaching a state of perfection but a mindset of continual improvement.

  Purpose: The need to be part of something larger than

ourselves. When personal and organizational purposes align, motivation and performance peak.

The Evolution of Motivation:

- **Motivation 1.0:** Survival. It's the basic biological drive.
- **Motivation 2.0:** Carrots and sticks. The reward and punishment approach, which Pink argues is increasingly outdated and ineffective.
- **Motivation 3.0:** The new paradigm which revolves around intrinsic motivation, where autonomy, mastery, and purpose are central.

The Flaws of Carrots & Sticks:

- Pink provides evidence that external rewards and punishments can be effective for routine, rule-based tasks but can diminish creativity and problem-solving skills for complex tasks.
- External rewards can extinguish intrinsic motivation, diminish performance

The Motivation Operating System:

- For the modern world, Pink suggests organizations should upgrade to Motivation 3.0, promoting autonomy, mastery, and purpose, to achieve better results and foster personal satisfaction.

Practical Recommendations:

- Pink offers various strategies to nurture intrinsic motivation, such as "FedEx Days" (where employees are given 24 hours to work on any project they choose) and "20% Time" (a concept employed by Google where engineers spend 20% of their time on projects of their choosing).

Why "Drive" is Essential Reading for Leaders and Individuals:

Daniel Pink's "Drive" reshapes the conversation about what truly motivates us, challenging age-old practices in business and education. By highlighting the limitations of extrinsic rewards and the transformative potential of intrinsic motivators, the book offers a roadmap for building more fulfilling personal and professional lives. For leaders, educators, and anyone interested in understanding human behavior, "Drive" provides compelling insights backed by rigorous research.

17

"Business Model Generation" by Alexander Osterwalder & Yves Pigneur

"Business Model Generation" introduces a unique and systematic approach to the conception, design, and analysis of business models. At the heart of this book is the Business Model Canvas, a visual framework that breaks down the nine fundamental building blocks of a business model.

The Business Model Canvas:

- **Channels:** How a company delivers its Value Proposition to customers.
- **Customer Relationships:** Defines the type of relationship a company establishes with its customers.
- **Revenue Streams:** Describes the way a company makes income from each Customer Segment.
- **Key Resources:** The critical assets required to operate and deliver the Value Proposition.
- **Key Activities:** The essential things a company must do to make its business model function.
- **Key Partnerships:** The external organizations, resources, or activities that a business relies on.
- **Cost Structure:** All costs involved in operating the business model.

Business Model Patterns:

- The book explores patterns of business models, such as "Unbundling Business Models," "The Long Tail," "Multi-Sided Platforms," and "Free as a Business Model," among others.

Design:

- Emphasizes the importance of design thinking and introduces techniques to visualize, prototype, and innovate business models.

Strategy:

- Discusses how business models are at the core of strategic management in the 21st century. It touches on blue ocean strategies and assessing the environment for threats and opportunities.

Process:

- Describes a comprehensive process, from understanding and analyzing to designing and implementing business models.

Outlook:

- A look into the future of business models, including topics like sustainability and technological advancements.

Why "Business Model Generation" is a Game-Changer for Entrepreneurs and Innovators:

"Business Model Generation" has garnered widespread acclaim for its innovative and

18

"The Effective Executive" by Peter F. Drucker

Peter F. Drucker's "The Effective Executive" is a classic in management literature, focusing on the behaviors and practices that define effective leadership. While the book acknowledges that intelligence, imagination, and knowledge are essential, it emphasizes that they are only useful if translated into actionable results. Drucker outlines several key practices that can ensure this translation occurs.

Effectiveness Can Be Learned:

· Drucker begins by emphasizing that effectiveness is a habit — a set of practices — that can and must be learned. It's not an innate talent, but a discipline.

Know Where Your Time Goes:

· Time is a precious and limited resource. Drucker advises executives to track their time, eliminate non-essential tasks, and delegate where possible. He underscores that effective executives do not begin with their tasks but with their time.

Focus on Outcomes:

- Effective executives focus on results, not effort. It's crucial to ask, "What can I contribute?" rather than just staying busy. This outward contribution focus is what differentiates effective executives from others.

Build on Strengths:

- Drucker argues that it's more productive to utilize strengths and neutralize weaknesses than to focus solely on improving weaknesses. This applies to both individuals and organizations. Effective executives also ensure that their own strengths are compatible with their job requirements.

Concentrate on a Few Major Areas:

perspectives are considered. He also highlights that every effective decision action needs to be followed by a 'feedback' to test the validity of the decision against the actual course of events.

Why "The Effective Executive" Remains Essential Reading for Leaders:

Peter F. Drucker's "The Effective Executive" stands the test of time by distilling timeless principles of leadership and productivity. While tools, technologies, and environments have evolved, the core tenets of decision-making, focusing on strengths, and managing one's time remain universally applicable. Drucker's clear and insightful prose offers actionable advice for leaders at all levels, making the book a staple in management literature.

19

"Solve for Happy" by Mo Gawdat

In "Solve for Happy," Mo Gawdat, a former Chief Business Officer for Google [X], takes a scientific and systematic approach to happiness. Drawing from his engineering background, he presents a model aiming to make the happiness equation more predictable and attainable.

The Happiness Equation:

include our perceptions of thought, self, knowledge, time, and control.

- By recognizing and understanding these illusions, we can recalibrate our perceptions to align more closely with reality.

Blind Spots:

- Just as illusions distort our perceptions, Gawdat argues that there are "blind spots" in our thinking which can skew our understanding of events. Recognizing these cognitive biases can help rectify our distortions.

Seven Ultimate Truths:

- Gawdat lists out truths that, when accepted, can lead to a more consistent state of happiness. These include the reality of now (living in the present), the impermanence of life, and the idea that change is the only constant.

Personal Tragedy and Perspective:

- Gawdat's motivation for the book and his exploration of happiness stems from personal tragedy. The unexpected death of his son spurred him on a journey to understand the nature of happiness and how it can be sustained even amidst profound pain.
- His perspective is both introspective and universally applicable, emphasizing that while pain is inevitable, suffering is optional.

6-7-5 Framework:

- **6** illusions that cloud our worldview.
- **7** blind spots that distort our perception of events.
- **5** ultimate truths that, when accepted, can lead to lasting happiness.

Why "Solve for Happy" Offers a Unique Perspective on Happiness:

Mo Gawdat's approach to happiness stands out for its fusion of logic, engineering principles, and personal introspection. His analytical method to deconstructing happiness aims to make the emotion more attainable and less elusive. For those who appreciate structured, logical approaches to life's intangibles, "Solve for Happy" provides a refreshing and insightful perspective. Furthermore, Gawdat's personal journey and vulnerability in sharing his own experiences lend the book a profound authenticity.

20

"Predictably Irrational" by Dan Ariely

"Predictably Irrational" explores the idea that humans are consistently and predictably irrational in their decisions, challenging the classic economic viewpoint that people always act rationally and in their best self-interest. Through a series of experiments and observations, behavioral economist Dan Ariely provides insights into why people make irrational decisions and how these tendencies influence various aspects of life.

The Cost of Zero Cost:

- Ariely discusses the allure of "free" and how it often leads us to make irrational choices. People are disproportionately excited about things that are free, even if they're not always the best options.

The Fallacy of Supply and Demand:

- Our first encounters with a product's price can anchor our perception of its value, leading us to make irrational purchasing decisions later. For instance, once we've paid a certain amount for coffee, we're likely to continue paying around that amount in the future, even if the coffee isn't worth that price.

The Cost of Social Norms:

- There's a difference between social exchanges (like favors among friends) and market exchanges (like paid services). Mixing the two, such as by paying someone for a previously social interaction, can result in negative outcomes.

The Influence of Arousal:

- People underestimate how much their decisions can be influenced by emotions, arousal, or other temporary states.

The Problem of Procrastination and Self-Control:

- Despite our best intentions, we often procrastinate or make decisions against our best interests.

- Our expectations, often influenced by price, can impact our actual experiences. For instance, if we believe a medication is expensive, we might believe it's more effective and actually experience more significant benefits.

Keeping Doors Open:

- People often prefer to keep options open, even at a cost, rather than commit to one path or decision. This can lead to missed opportunities and less satisfaction.

The Effect of Expectations:

- If we expect something to be a certain way, our experience can align with those expectations, even if the reality is different.

The Context of Our Character:

- How we view our own honesty and the honesty of others can be influenced by various factors, from the chance to benefit personally to the distance we feel from the act itself.

Why "Predictably Irrational" is a Must-Read for Decision Makers:

Dan Ariely's "Predictably Irrational" uncovers the quirks and biases in human decision-making, offering readers insights into their own behavior and the behavior of those around them. For anyone involved in business, design, policy-making, or simply interested in understanding the intricacies of human behavior, the book provides valuable lessons. Ariely's engaging storytelling, combined with thorough research, makes complex behavioral economics concepts accessible and relatable.

21

"Purple Cow" by Seth Godin

"Purple Cow" is Seth Godin's call-to-action for businesses to stand out in an overcrowded marketplace. The central metaphor of the book revolves around the idea that if you were driving past a field of cows, a purple cow would stand out immediately. In the same way, businesses need to be remarkable to be noticed.

The Old Marketing Model is Broken:

- Godin argues that traditional methods of marketing (TV ads, billboards, etc.) have become less effective due to over-saturation. He calls this mass advertising the "TV-Industrial Complex" and asserts that it no longer guarantees success as it once might have.

Being Safe is Risky:

- Contrary to popular belief, playing it safe and creating products that appeal to the masses can be the riskiest strategy. Such products often fade into obscurity. On the other hand, creating something unique and targeting a niche can lead to more significant success.

The Importance of Remarkability:

- A "Purple Cow" is anything phenomenal, counterintuitive, exciting—essentially, something worth making a remark about. Remarkable doesn't mean extravagant or luxury; it means worth talking about.

Targeting the Innovators and Early Adopters:

- Godin emphasizes the importance of the "early adopters" or those who are eager to try something new. By targeting these individuals, businesses can create a dedicated fan base that spreads the word and markets the product.

Designing for a Niche:

- Instead of trying to app

Creating the Cow:

- The latter part of the book delves into how businesses can foster creativity and innovation to develop their own "Purple Cow." This involves encouraging new ideas, taking calculated risks, and being willing to fail.

Why "Purple Cow" is a Valuable Read for Entrepreneurs and Marketers:

Seth Godin's "Purple Cow" is a concise, engaging read that challenges conventional business wisdom. In an era where consumers are bombarded with advertisements and choices, standing out is more crucial than ever. Godin's emphasis on the power of being remarkable and focusing on niches can provide businesses with a roadmap to success in the modern age. His insights, backed by a multitude of examples, showcase the importance of innovation and boldness in today's business landscape.

22

"The Four Steps to the Epiphany" by Steve Blank

Steve Blank's "The Four Steps to the Epiphany" is a seminal work in the realm of startups and entrepreneurship, which introduced the idea of "Customer Development," a structured approach to building startups and launching new products. This methodology contrasts with the traditional product development model and emphasizes customer feedback and iterative design.

- **Customer Discovery:** This is the phase where entrepreneurs validate that a market for their product exists. It involves understanding customer problems, needs, and challenges. The aim is to ascertain whether the solution being created aligns with market needs.
- **Customer Validation:** Here, the entrepreneur aims to build a repeatable sales model. This phase is about ensuring that the product is something customers genuinely want and are willing to pay for.
- **Customer Creation:** This phase is about creating end-user demand and driving that demand into the company's sales channel. It's where strategies for positioning, sales, and marketing are defined and scaled.
- **Company Building:** Once a valid business model is established, the focus shifts from merely finding customers to building a company that can execute the business model. This transition involves moving from a startup to a company optimized for executing under a known business model.

Minimum Viable Product (MVP):

- Before this book, the emphasis was often on creating a complete product before launch. Blank introduced the idea of an MVP—a version of the product that allows for the maximum amount of validated learning about customers with the least effort.

Iterative Approach:

- A key tenet of Blank's methodology is iteration. Based on

feedback during the Customer Discovery and Validation phases, startups may need to "pivot" (make a fundamental change to the product) or "proceed" (continue with the established course).

The Importance of Getting Out of the Building:

- A repeated phrase and theme in the book is "get out of the building." Blank stresses that true learning doesn't occur inside the confines of a startup's office but out in the field, interacting with real customers.

Why "The Four Steps to the Epiphany" is Crucial for Startups:

Steve Blank's methodology, as laid out in this book, was revolutionary when first introduced and remains foundational in the startup world. His emphasis on understanding customers' needs and iterating based on real-world feedback has saved countless startups from the pitfalls of building products in a vacuum. The book has directly influenced the L

23

"Who Moved My Cheese?" by Dr. Spencer Johnson

"Who Moved My Cheese?" is a motivational business fable that explores how different individuals deal with change in their personal and professional lives. The narrative is set in a maze, where four characters search for "cheese" that represents happiness, success, or whatever one desires in life.

The Characters:

- **Sniff:** Detects change early and quickly adapts to it. He sniffs out the situation and anticipates when he needs to move with the cheese.
- **Scurry:** Doesn't overthink or overanalyze—when change happens, he quickly scurries into action.
- **Hem:** Dislikes change and fears the unknown. He resists change and wishes for things to return to how they were.
- **Haw:** Initially hesitant about change, but he learns to embrace it over time. He understands that moving with the cheese leads to new opportunities.

The Story:

Initially, all characters enjoy a constant supply of cheese. But one day, the cheese is moved. Sniff and Scurry quickly move on to find new cheese, while Hem and Haw stay behind, upset about the change and hoping the cheese will return. Over time, Haw realizes the need to move on and starts looking for new cheese, while Hem remains resistant and stuck in his ways.

Key Lessons:

- **Anticipate Change:** Be prepared for the cheese to move, as change is a natural part of life.
- **Adapt to Change Quickly:** The quicker you let go of the old cheese (old ways or past success), the sooner you can enjoy the new.
- **Enjoy Change:** Embrace the adventure of finding new cheese.
- **Be Ready to Change Again and Again:** Keep moving with the cheese and stay agile.

Dr. Spencer Johnson's fable has gained worldwide acclaim for its universal message about life's inevitability: change. The book serves as a simple, yet profound, guide for dealing with change positively. Its lessons resonate with individuals and organizations alike, as everyone faces change—whether by choice or circumstance. The allegory encourages a proactive mindset, adaptability, and the willingness to leave one's comfort zone.

24

"Think and Grow Rich" by Napoleon Hill

"Think and Grow Rich" is one of the best-selling books of all time, having sold over 100 million copies. Napoleon Hill penned it in 1937 after interviewing numerous successful individuals over two decades, including Andrew Carnegie, Thomas Edison, and Henry Ford. The book condenses these findings into principles that can lead to personal and financial success.

Desire:

Autosuggestion:

- The principle involves regularly feeding one's subconscious mind with affirmations or repeated statements of one's goals, thus leading the mind toward the achievement of those goals.

Specialized Knowledge:

- General knowledge, per se, is not as potent as specialized knowledge. The key is to acquire knowledge in your specific domain of interest and put it into practical use.

Imagination:

- The imagination, especially the creative imagination, is the workshop wherein all plans are created. It's essential to dream and visualize what you desire.

Organized Planning:

- Wishing won't make you rich. You need clear plans that are both actionable and flexible.

Decision:

- Procrastination is the enemy of success. Successful people make decisions quickly and change them slowly.

Persistence:

- Persistence is crucial for turning your desires into reality. Overcoming obstacles and continuing despite failures is a common trait among successful individuals.

Power of the Master Mind:

- Surrounding oneself with a group of like-minded individuals or a team can multiply one's efforts and insights. Collaboration often results in synergy.

The Mystery of Sex Transmutation:

- Hill touches upon channeling sexual energy into efforts that contribute to success, stating that many successful people have a high sexual drive which they harness in productive ways.

The Subconscious Mind:

- Positive and negative emotions can't occupy the mind simultaneously. D

- Sometimes referred to as intuition or gut feeling, this principle is about trusting those flashes of inspiration or hunches.

Overcoming Fear:

- Hill identifies six primary fears: poverty, criticism, ill health, loss of love, old age, and death. Recognizing and addressing these fears is crucial for success.

Why "Think and Grow Rich" Remains an Essential Read:

"Think and Grow Rich" isn't just about financial wealth; it's a guide to cultivating the mindset and habits that lead to success in any endeavor. Its timeless principles, built on decades of observations of successful individuals, offer a roadmap to personal achievement. The book emphasizes the idea that thoughts can shape one's reality, making it a foundational read in the self-help and personal development genre.

25

"Secrets of the Millionaire Mind" by T. Harv Eker

T. Harv Eker's "Secrets of the Millionaire Mind" delves into the foundational psychological elements that underpin wealth creation and retention. Eker posits that everyone has a personal money blueprint ingrained in their subconscious mind, which determines their financial success.

Your Money Blueprint:

believe "Life happens to me."
- **Rich people play the money game to win**, but poor people play the money game not to lose.
- **Rich people think big**, whereas poor people think small.
- **Rich people focus on opportunities**; poor people focus on obstacles.

The Process of Manifestation:

- Eker describes the process of manifestation as: "Thoughts lead to feelings. Feelings lead to actions. Actions lead to results." To change our financial situation, we need to change our thinking.

The Power of Declarations:

- Eker encourages the reader to use positive affirmations or "declarations" to influence their subconscious mind and reshape their financial blueprint.

Taking Responsibility:

- One of the key themes of the book is taking complete responsibility for one's financial circumstances. Complaining and blaming are antithetical to wealth accumulation.

Net Worth Statement and Financial Tracking:

- Eker emphasizes the importance of knowing where you stand financially. Regularly tracking income, expenses, assets, and liabilities is crucial for financial success.

The Importance of Passive Income:

- He stresses the value of building sources of passive income and making your money work for you.

Why "Secrets of the Millionaire Mind" is a Noteworthy Read on Wealth Mindset:

T. Harv Eker provides insights into the subconscious beliefs that can either propel us to financial success or hold us back. The book challenges readers to introspect on their existing beliefs about money, comparing them to the "wealth files" and then to take actionable steps towards reshaping detrimental patterns of thought. Its principles don't just apply to financial wealth but can be used to achieve success in other areas of life as well.

26

"Scaling Up" by Verne Harnish

"Scaling Up" serves as a guide for businesses that are past the startup phase and are now grappling with the challenges of scaling. Harnish, also known as the "Growth Guy," builds on the principles from his previous work, "Mastering the Rockefeller Habits," and provides a comprehensive framework that companies can use to grow successfully. The book is divided into four key areas: People, Strategy, Execution, and Cash.

People:

· It's imperative to have the right individuals on board to ensure growth. This means not just hiring for talent, but also for cultural fit. Harnish presents tools and techniques to manage, motivate, and maintain a high-performing team.

Strategy:

- For successful scaling, a robust and coherent strategy is paramount. This section delves into differentiating your company, defining its core values, and creating a unique selling proposition (USP). The aim is to drive both profitability and passion in the business.

Execution:

- Even the best strategies are meaningless without excellent execution. Harnish provides tools to improve operations, maintain consistent quality, and ensure that the entire company is aligned and moving cohesively towards its goals. It emphasizes the importance of daily and weekly rhythms, KPIs, and meeting structures to maintain momentum.

Cash:

- Cash flow is the lifeblood of a growing company. The book outlines strategies for generating cash, optimizing its use, and ensuring that there's always sufficient liquidity to support

The One-Page Strategic Plan:

· One of the book's hallmarks is the One-Page Strategic Plan (OPSP), a tool to keep the entire company aligned. This single-page document distills the company's mission, values, goals, and priorities, ensuring everyone is on the same page.

Why "Scaling Up" is Essential Reading for Growing Companies:

"Scaling Up" offers actionable tools and frameworks, backed by real-world examples, that businesses can implement immediately. Harnish's approach is practical and grounded, focusing on the core elements a company needs to master for successful growth. The book isn't just theory—it's a hands-on manual that answers the crucial question many business leaders face: "How can we grow without losing the essence of what made us successful in the first place?"

27

"Built to Sell" by John Warrillow

"Built to Sell" is a narrative about an entrepreneur named Alex Stapleton who runs a marketing agency but struggles with the business's demands and unpredictability. With the guidance of his mentor, Ted, Alex transforms his service business into a sellable company. Through this parable, Warrillow imparts essential principles that every business owner should consider if they ever hope to sell their enterprise.

Specialize to Differentiate

consistent delivery, regardless of who's managing the operation.

Remove the Owner from Operations:

- For a business to be sellable, it should operate smoothly without the owner's constant involvement. This means training employees, building teams, and delegating responsibilities effectively.

Build Recurring Revenue Streams:

- Predictable, recurring revenue makes a business more attractive to potential buyers. This could be achieved through subscription models, retainers, or any form of consistent income.

Avoid the Trap of Customization:

- Customizing products or services for individual clients can make a business hard to scale and less attractive to buyers. Standardization is key.

Create a Positive Cash Flow Cycle:

- A business that generates cash (e.g., by getting customers to pay upfront) is more valuable than one that burns cash.

Hire Salespeople:

- Instead of relying solely on the owner's personal relationships for sales, hire sales teams to institutionalize and scale the process.

Avoid the Single Point of Failure:

- Ensure that no single client makes up a significant portion of your revenue. Diversify the client base to reduce risks.

Maintain Your Documentation:

- Standard operating procedures, employee handbooks, and other key documents should be maintained. These demonstrate to potential buyers that the business can run without the owner.

Know When to Sell:

- Timing is crucial. Owners should be mindful of market conditions, industry trends, and personal circumstances to determine the optimal time to sell.

28

"The 10X Rule" by Grant Cardone

"The 10X Rule" posits a straightforward but transformative concept: to achieve extraordinary results, individuals must commit to setting goals that are ten times bigger than what they initially believe they can achieve, and then take actions that are ten times greater than they think necessary.

The Premise of Underestimation:

- Cardone starts by addressing a common misconception: that most failures arise from taking excessive action. In reality, most shortcomings result from grossly underestimating the amount of effort and action necessary to achieve a particular goal. This underestimation leads to lower targets and insufficient actions.

Four Degrees of Action:

- Cardone categorizes action into four levels:
- **No Action:** Complete inactivity and passivity.

- **Retreat:** Actions that pull you back from your goals.
- **Average Action:** The standard level at which most people operate, often leading to ordinary results.
- **Massive Action:** The level required to achieve outstanding results and to realize the 10X goals.

Expanding the Comfort Zone:

- Operating at 10X levels often means moving well beyond one's comfort zone. The majority operate within this zone, leading to mediocrity. However, extraordinary results require venturing into territories of uncertainty and discomfort.

Embracing Fear and Criticism:

- As individuals elevate their goals and take massive actions, they will undoubtedly encounter fear and criticism. Rather than being deterrents, Cardone views these as indicators of being on the right track. It's vital to anticipate these a negative trait. A 10X mindset requires an all-consuming passion for the goals set, making the pursuit almost an obsession.

Sustained Efforts:

- Initial momentum is not enough. The 10X rule demands sustained massive actions. This means continuous engagement, re-evaluation, and recalibration of efforts to ensure alignment with the overarching goals.

Avoiding the Traps of Success:

- Complacency is the enemy of further achievement. Even when one attains a certain level of success, it's essential to continue operating at 10X levels to avoid stagnation or regression.

Significance of "The 10X Rule":

Cardone's "The 10X Rule" isn't just another self-help book. It's a challenge, a call to action, and a wakeup call for those who seek extraordinary achievements. It underscores the idea that average efforts can only lead to average outcomes. For those who desire to rise above the norm, rethink their potential, and truly make an impact, the 10X mindset is not just beneficial—it's imperative.

29

"Oversubscribed" by Daniel Priestley

"Oversubscribed" is a guide for businesses and entrepreneurs to generate demand greater than supply for their products or services, thus making them 'oversubscribed.' Priestley presents a combination of practical strategies and principles to achieve this status.

Oversubscription Principle:

- At the core of the book is the

create an oversubscribed business.

Understanding Cycles and Campaigns:

- Businesses should operate in a rhythm or cycle, not continuously. This means having distinct phases: research, development, pre-launch, launch, and delivery. By focusing on campaigns, businesses can create spikes in demand.

Knowing Your Capacity:

- It's vital to know your business's capacity. This isn't just about quantity, but about the number of clients or customers you can deliver exceptional value to.

The Power of Market Intelligence:

- Before trying to be oversubscribed, understand your market deeply. This involves knowing what people want, why they want it, and how they consume it.

Building a Tribe:

- Create a community or tribe around your brand. Your tribe should consist of passionate followers, clients, and fans who advocate for you. They help in creating buzz and demand.

Turning Customers into Ambassadors:

- Deliver exceptional value, and your customers become

ambassadors. Their testimonials, word-of-mouth, and advocacy can be more effective than traditional advertising.

Creating a Memorable Market Proposition:

- Your market should not just know you; they should remember you. This requires a unique value proposition and a memorable way to present it.

Pricing Strategy:

- Being oversubscribed allows for a dynamic pricing strategy. When demand is high, prices can be premium. This not only increases profitability but also enhances the perceived value.

Effective Communication:

- Regularly communicate your unique value, the successes of your clients, and why you're different. Use stories and narratives that shift. Rather than chasing clients or constantly hunting for business, the goal is to create an environment where clients are hunting for you. Through a mix of strategic planning, market insight, and value delivery, businesses can reach a point where they're not just sought after, but are genuinely oversubscribed. It's a model that ensures sustainability, profitability, and growth in a world where attention is the most coveted commodity.

30

"Atomic Habits" by James Clear

"Atomic Habits" is a synthesis of James Clear's meticulous research on habit formation, coupled with engaging stories and practical advice on how one can transform habits to achieve personal and professional goals.

Habits: Tiny But Mighty:

- Clear starts with the idea that habits are like atoms: tiny and seemingly insignificant but

- The principle of making a 1% improvement daily can lead to significant positive changes over time. Conversely, decreasing by 1% can lead you down a spiral of negative outcomes.

The Four Laws of Behavior Change:

- Clear defines a set of "laws" to build new habits and break bad ones:

1. **Make It Obvious:** Be clear about what you want to achieve and set up your environment to trigger desired behaviors.
2. **Make It Attractive:** Use temptation bundling and positive reinforcement to make good habits feel rewarding.
3. **Make It Easy:** Reduce the steps and effort required to perform the habit. The two-minute rule is a tool here: if it takes less than two minutes, do it now.
4. **Make It Satisfying:** Ensure immediate satisfaction from the habit, which reinforces its recurrence.
5. **Inversion of the Four Laws:**

- To break bad habits, invert the four laws:

1. Make it Invisible.
2. Make it Unattractive.
3. Make it Difficult.
4. Make it Unsatisfying.

Identity-Based Habits:

- Long term habit formation is more effective when rooted

in one's identity. For instance, instead of "I want to read," adopt "I am a reader." This shift in self-perception drives behavior more consistently.

The Role of the Environment:

- Clear emphasizes the role of a conducive environment in habit formation. An environment that aligns with your goals can make good habits effortless and bad habits impossible.

Habit Tracking and Accountability:

- Monitoring progress is crucial. Habit tracking, whether through apps, journals, or other means, makes you accountable and provides the satisfaction of marking progress.

Embracing the Plateau:

- Mastery requires patience. Clear discusses the "Plateau of Latent Po...

Significance of "Atomic Habits":

James Clear's "Atomic Habits" redefines how we think about progress and success. By emphasizing the power of compound growth, he provides a roadmap to transform minuscule changes into remarkable results. Beyond just a manual for habit change, it's a guide to rethinking one's identity, refining processes, and recognizing the latent potential within tiny, consistent efforts.

31

"They Ask, You Answer" by Marcus Sheridan

"They Ask, You Answer" is a content marketing methodology rooted in transparency, helpfulness, and a customer-centric approach. Marcus Sheridan, once a struggling pool business owner, shares how he transformed his business by directly addressing his customers' questions online. The book presents a roadmap for businesses to gain trust, build authority, and drive sales by genuinely addressing customer inquiries.

cess. Today's consumers do their research online, often completing 70% or more of their buying decision before ever contacting a salesperson. Businesses must adapt to this change by meeting customers in their research phase.

The Five Subjects Businesses Don't Like to Talk About:

· Sheridan identifies five topics that companies tend to avoid but are crucial to customers: Pricing, Problems (comparing negatives), Comparisons, Reviews, and "Best in Class." Addressing these transparently can set a company apart.

Content is the Key:

· Businesses should consider themselves as media companies. This means continually producing content (blogs, videos, podcasts) that address customer questions and concerns.

The 80% Video Rule:

· Sheridan champions video content. He suggests that businesses should aim to answer 80% of customer questions through video, given its engagement and retention rates.

Sales Teams as Teachers:

· The sales process should be educational. By teaching prospective customers, sales teams can position themselves as consultative partners rather than just transactional vendors

Content Saturation Index:

- This is a method to assess how well a company has covered crucial topics within their industry. The goal is to be the definitive source of information in your niche.

Inbound Marketing:

- Embrace inbound marketing tactics, where potential clients come to you based on the value you provide, rather than traditional outbound strategies like cold calling.

User Experience and Design:

- The website's design, speed, and overall user experience play a vital role. If users can't find answers quickly, they'll leave.

HubSpot and Content Management:

- Sheridan touches upon the imp... of... like

importance of transparency, education, and adapting to the modern buyer's journey. It presents a compelling case that in the age of information, companies can no longer afford to be secretive or evasive. By addressing customer inquiries head-on, businesses can position themselves as industry leaders, gain customer trust, and drive significant sales growth.

32

"Fanatical Prospecting" by Jeb Blount

"Fanatical Prospecting" serves as a guide to the most essential aspect of sales: prospecting. Jeb Blount emphasizes that consistent and persistent prospecting is vital for filling the sales pipeline and thus, for any salesperson's success. Through this book, Blount offers techniques, strategies, and insights into the art and discipline of effective prospecting.

The Importance of Prospecting:

prospecting.

The 5 C's of Social Selling:

- Blount discusses the integration of social media into prospecting with the five C's: Connect, Converse, Convert, Collaborate, and Close. Each step outlines how to engage potential leads through social channels, from initiating conversations to closing deals.

Balancing Inbound and Outbound:

- While inbound leads (those that come to you) are valuable, they cannot replace active outbound prospecting. Blount argues for a balanced approach, leveraging both strategies.

The Law of Replacement:

- A salesperson must always be adding new prospects to replace the ones that inevitably drop out of the pipeline. This law underlines the relentless nature of prospecting.

Phone Prospecting Tips:

- Blount offers a variety of strategies for effective phone prospecting. This includes techniques for getting past gatekeepers, handling objections, and making impactful first impressions.

Email Prospecting:

- In today's digital age, email prospecting is crucial. Blount offers insights on crafting compelling subject lines, keeping emails concise, and making strong calls to action.

The Three Ps:

- Persistence, Patience, and Perseverance are emphasized as the essential qualities of a successful prospector.

Managing Rejection:

- Salespeople face rejection regularly. Blount provides strategies for handling rejection, maintaining a positive mindset, and moving forward without getting discouraged.

Daily Routines and Disciplines:

- A structured daily routine is vital for effective prospecting. Blount recommends setting aside dedicated blocks of time for prospecting activities and minimizing distractions.

results.

33

"The Tipping Point" by Malcolm Gladwell

"The Tipping Point" delves into how small changes can trigger a 'tipping point' or a dramatic moment of critical mass, leading to significant and sometimes societal-level effects. Malcolm Gladwell provides a deep dive into the phenomena that go viral, whether it's the rise in popularity of a product, the spread of a trend, or the outbreak of a social behavior.

Three Rules of Epid...

- **Power of Context:** Human behavior is sensitive to and strongly influenced by the environment or context. Even small changes in context can have a dramatic effect on an epidemic's tipping point.

Yawning is Contagious:

- Gladwell uses the analogy of a yawn to explain how ideas and behaviors spread. Just as seeing someone yawn can cause another person to yawn, witnessing certain behaviors or encountering particular ideas can cause them to spread virally.

The Magic Number 150:

- Referring to Dunbar's number, Gladwell discusses how there's a limit to the number of people with whom one can maintain genuine social relationships. This number is approximately 150, and it has significance in creating effective networks and communities.

Blue's Clues and Sesame Street:

- Gladwell examines children's television shows like "Blue's Clues" and "Sesame Street" to demonstrate the stickiness factor. These programs captivated children by understanding and leveraging cognitive tools that made their content 'sticky' and memorable.

The Rise of Hush Puppies:

- As a case study, Gladwell recounts the resurgence in popularity of Hush Puppies shoes in the 1990s. The brand had reached a tipping point because of the specific individuals who began wearing them, leading to a massive revival.

The Spread of Syphilis:

- Analyzing the syphilis epidemic in Baltimore, Gladwell demonstrates how the power of context, including external conditions and cultural environments, can lead to sudden and unexpected changes in behavior.

Broken Windows Theory:

- Gladwell discusses the theory that suggests that visible signs of disorder and neglect can lead to an increase in crime. Addressing small problems, like fixing broken windows, can create a context that prevents more significant problems.

34

"The One Minute Manager" by Kenneth Blanchard & Spencer Johnson

"The One Minute Manager" presents a concise, easily under-stood management style based on three fundamental tech-niques. Written as a parable, the book recounts the journey of a young man seeking the best manager and the lessons he learns.

One Minute Goals:

- The essence here is to ensure that responsibilities are clear from the beginning. Employees should be able to review their responsibilities in 60 seconds. This clarity allows individuals to understand what's expected and how their performance will be evaluated.
- Managers should work with their team members to define and agree upon clear goals and write them down, each taking no longer than a minute to read.
- By keeping goals concise and clear, team members can frequently revisit them, ensuring they stay on track.

One Minute Praisings:

- Instead of waiting for a formal review to provide feedback, managers should catch their employees doing something right and immediately praise them.
- The steps involve: telling people upfront that you'll be letting them know how they're doing; when you see good behavior or performance, delivering specific praise; and then pausing to allow the person to 'feel' the praise, reinforcing the positive impact of their actions.
- By giving immediate and positive feedback, managers reinforce desired behaviors and outcomes, making it more likely that such behaviors will be repeated in the future.

One Minute Reprimands:

- When an employee does something wrong, a manager should provide immediate feedback. The reprimand should be specific and address the behavior, not the person.
- The process involves telling individuals what they did wrong, how you f...

"The One Minute Manager" champions simplicity in management. Blanchard and Johnson argue that effective management doesn't need to be complicated or time-consuming. The three one-minute tools presented in the book can lead to improved productivity, job satisfaction, and personal prosperity. By focusing on clear communication and maintaining the human element, the One Minute Manager techniques emphasize the importance of both results and people.

35

"Crossing the Chasm" by Geoffrey A. Moore

"Crossing the Chasm" is a seminal work that addresses the challenges startup companies face when transitioning from early adopters to mainstream customers. Geoffrey A. Moore explores the difficulties tech startups encounter when moving from the initial niche markets to broader markets and offers strategies to successfully navigate this "chasm."

Technology Ad

4. Late Majority: Skeptics who are cautious about innovations.

5. Laggards: The last group to adopt an innovation.

The Chasm:

· Between the Early Adopters and the Early Majority lies the 'chasm.' This gap represents a significant challenge as the needs and expectations of early adopters vary greatly from the early majority. Many startups falter when trying to cross this chasm because they fail to transition from serving a niche market (early adopters) to the broader market (early majority).

Whole Product Concept:

· To appeal to the mainstream market, companies must offer a 'whole product' — a comprehensive solution that caters to the customer's needs. While early adopters might be satisfied with a promising but incomplete product, the early majority expects a complete solution.

Targeting the Beachhead:

· Moore recommends that companies focus on a niche segment (a 'beachhead') within the early majority. By dominating this niche, companies can establish a strong position and reference base, making it easier to expand to adjacent markets.

Positioning:

- It's essential to communicate the product's value proposition clearly. Moore advocates for creating a positioning statement that details the product, its primary competition, its target market, and the unique benefits it offers.

Creating the Bowling Alley:

- Once the beachhead is secured, companies can tackle adjacent market segments, like how pins fall in a bowling alley. Each segment should be approached based on its unique needs.

Tornado, Main Street, and End of Life:

- After crossing the chasm, Moore describes a 'tornado' phase where mass-market consumers rush to buy the product. This is followed by the 'Main Street' phase, where growth stabilizes, and finally, the 'End of Life' phase when the market matures and growth plateaus.

36

"Rich Dad Poor Dad" by Robert T. Kiyosaki

"Rich Dad Poor Dad" is Robert T. Kiyosaki's personal journey into financial understanding, presented through the contrasting advice of two father figures. One, his biological father (referred to as "Poor Dad"), emphasizes traditional education and a steady job. The other, the father of a childhood friend (referred to as "Rich Dad"), offers insights into wealth-building and financial independence.

The Importance of Financial Literacy:

· Kiyosaki stresses the significance of understanding finances, including the ability to read and understand financial statements. Being financially literate is key to making informed decisions about money.

Assets vs. Liabilities:

· One of the book's core principles is the distinction between assets and liabilities. In Kiyosaki's terms, assets put money into your pocket, and liabilities take money out. The wealthy buy assets, while the poor and middle class often accumulate liabilities thinking they are assets.

The Rat Race:

- Kiyosaki describes how many people get caught in a cycle of working for money instead of having money work for them. By prioritizing high salaries, promotions, and job security, they increase their expenses with each raise, perpetuating a cycle of working to support their lifestyle.

Importance of Entrepreneurship:

- Rather than relying solely on a traditional job and salary, Kiyosaki champions entrepreneurship and investing as paths to financial independence. He emphasizes the need to take calculated risks and learn from failures.

Overcoming

financial matters. Mistakes are opportunities to learn.

Seeking Opportunities:

· The rich don't wait for opportunities to come to them; they actively seek and create them. Investing in real estate, building businesses, and leveraging market opportunities are ways the wealthy build their assets.

Significance of "Rich Dad Poor Dad":

"Rich Dad Poor Dad" has been lauded for its approach to financial education, particularly its emphasis on financial independence and building wealth through investing in assets. Kiyosaki's lessons, derived from the contrasting advice of his two "dads," challenge conventional beliefs about money, work, and life. While some critics argue that the book oversimplifies complex financial strategies and lacks detailed actionable steps, its principles have resonated with many seeking an alternative perspective on money and investing.

37

"The Black Swan" by Nassim Nicholas Taleb

"The Black Swan" delves into the impact of highly improbable events on the world and our inability to predict them. Nassim Nicholas Taleb coins these events "Black Swans," using the metaphor of the discovery of black swans in Australia — a surprising occurrence given that all swans in the Old World were believed to be white.

Definition f Bl

- Taleb argues that much of what happens in the world is random and unknowable in advance. Human beings, however, have a tendency to seek patterns, construct narratives, and simplify complex phenomena, which often leads to overconfidence in predictions and underestimation of risks.

The Problem with "Mediocristan" and "Extremistan":

- Taleb contrasts two fictional realms: "Mediocristan" and "Extremistan." In Mediocristan, when you sample more data, outliers don't significantly affect the aggregate or total (e.g., human height or weight). In Extremistan, however, outliers or exceptional variables can dramatically shift the total (e.g., wealth distribution). Many modern phenomena belong to Extremistan, yet many predictive models treat them as if they belong to Mediocristan, leading to significant errors.

The Ludic Fallacy:

- Taleb introduces the concept of the "Ludic Fallacy," which refers to the mistake of assuming that structured, predictable models (often found in games) can be applied seamlessly to understand complex, unstructured realities.

Scalability:

- In professions or domains where scalability is possible, small numbers of individuals or events can dominate the entire distribution. For instance, one book out of millions becomes a bestseller, or a few tech companies dominate the market.

Domains of Applicability:

· While Black Swans are prevalent in economics, finance, and technology due to their scalable nature, they are less frequent in domains where variability is limited, like car accidents or mortality rates.

Robustification and Antifragility:

· While Black Swans can't be predicted, societies and systems can be made more robust or even "antifragile" — a term Taleb elaborates on more in his subsequent book, implying that they benefit or grow stronger from shocks and volatility.

Significance of "The Black Swan":

38

"Profit First" by Mike Michalowicz

"Profit First" turns traditional accounting practices on their head by challenging the age-old formula: Sales - Expenses = Profit. Instead, Michalowicz posits that a new formula, Sales - Profit = Expenses, can revolutionize any business, ensuring profitability from the outset.

Traditional vs. Profit First Approach:

- Traditionally, business owners prioritize expenses, leaving profit as an afterthought or "what's left." Michalowicz's approach dictates that profit is taken first, automatically ensuring profitability and forcing businesses to adapt by running on the remaining amount.

The Bank Balance Accounting Reality:

- Recognizing that many small business owners manage their finances based on their bank balance rather than detailed accounting reports, Michalowicz builds on this reality. By structuring bank accounts strategically, owners can get a clear and immediate snapshot of where their money is and allocate it appropriately.

Setting Up the System:

- The core strategy involves setting up multiple bank accounts for specific purposes: Income, Profit, Owner's Compensation, Tax, and Operating Expenses. By allocating percentages of income to each account regularly, business owners create a system where each dollar has a purpose.

Tackling Debt and Expenses:

- With the Profit First approach, expenses must fit within the constraints of what's left after profit and other allocations. This structure prompts businesses to reconsider and reduce unnecessary expenses and prioritize cost-effective strategies. If a company has debt, Michalowicz suggests leveraging the profit account to systematically eliminate it.

income to allocate to each account. These percentages are tailored based on the company's revenue, but the objective remains to gradually increase the profit percentage over time.

Addressing Challenges:

· Implementing Profit First may initially present some challenges, especially if current expenses exceed available funds after allocations. However, Michalowicz encourages businesses to see this as an opportunity to innovate, renegotiate costs, or cut unnecessary expenditures.

Significance of "Profit First":

"Profit First" offers a straightforward and actionable system that emphasizes the importance of profitability in business. By reshaping how business owners think about profit and expenses, Michalowicz's method aims to eradicate entrepreneurial poverty and ensure financial health. The book has been lauded for its pragmatic approach and its potential to transform businesses of any size.

39

"The Art of Possibility" by Rosamund Stone Zander & Benjamin Zander

"The Art of Possibility" offers a transformative perspective on life, work, and relationships through a combination of personal stories, parables, and practical advice. The Zanders — Rosamund, a therapist and landscape painter, and Benjamin, the conductor of the Boston Philharmonic — integrate their experiences to present a unique approach to unleashing creativity, passion, and productivity.

- Rather than seeing oneself as a fixed point or competing in a limited world (the "world of measurement"), one should envision a vast realm of possibilities and growth.

Giving an A:

- Drawing from Benjamin's experience as a teacher, they discuss the idea of "giving an A" to students on the first day of class. This is not about lowering standards but about approaching others with an assumption of their potential, thereby allowing them to envision their best selves.

Being a Contribution:

- Instead of operating with success and failure in mind, the Zanders advocate for an approach centered on contribution. This shift from scarcity to abundance allows individuals to see their actions as gifts and genuinely make a difference.

Leading from Any Chair:

- Leadership isn't just for those in designated positions of authority. Everyone has the potential to lead and inspire, regardless of their role.

Rule Number 6 (Don't Take Yourself So Seriously):

- The Zanders emphasize the importance of lightness and humor. By not taking ourselves too seriously, we can navigate challenges more effectively and joyfully.

The Way Things Are:

- Accepting the current reality without resistance — seeing "the way things are" — is foundational for discovering new possibilities.

Giving Way to Passion:

- Letting go of old resentments and barriers can reignite our innate passions. The Zanders encourage readers to pursue what genuinely moves them.

Creating Frameworks for Possibility:

- Instead of getting trapped in negativity, we can ask questions that create a structure for positive outcomes, such as "What assumption am I making, that I'm not aware I'm making, that gives me what I see?"

Telling the 'WE' Story:

of insights that inspire readers to shed limiting beliefs and embrace a world of endless potential. Their collaborative work serves as a testament to the transformative power of perspective, creativity, and human connection.

40

"Competitive Strategy" by Michael E. Porter

"Competitive Strategy: Techniques for Analyzing Industries and Competitors" is a seminal work in the world of business strategy. Published in 1980, the book, written by Michael E. Porter, a professor at Harvard Business School, introduced groundbreaking concepts that have since shaped the way businesses approach competition and strategic thinking.

The Five Forces Fr

of products outside the realm of the common product boundaries increases the propensity of customers to switch to alternatives.

- **Bargaining Power of Buyers:** Powerful buyers can exert pressure to drive down prices or increase product quality.
- **Bargaining Power of Suppliers:** Powerful suppliers can raise prices or reduce product quality.

Generic Competitive Strategies:

- Porter outlines three main strategies businesses can adopt to achieve and sustain a competitive advantage:
- **Cost Leadership:** Achieving the lowest cost of production and delivery in the industry.
- **Differentiation:** Offering unique products or services that are valued by customers.
- **Focus (or Niche Strategy):** Tailoring efforts to serve a particular segment or niche of the market better than competitors.

Value Chain Analysis:

- Beyond the generic strategies, Porter introduces the concept of the value chain. Every firm is a collection of activities that are executed to design, produce, market, deliver, and support its products. By analyzing these activities, firms can determine where they can create value.

Strategic Decisions and Trade-offs:

- Companies must make trade-offs in competing. They must

choose what not to do and avoid "stuck in the middle" status, where they neither differentiate nor achieve cost leadership.

Forecasting Industry Evolution and Changes:

- Understanding how an industry might evolve is crucial. Porter discusses the product life cycle and how industry factors change as industries mature.

Strategic Groups within Industries:

- Not all competitors in an industry are equally relevant. Firms can be grouped into strategic groups based on key similarities, and rivalry is typically stronger between firms that are within the same strategic group.

Competitive Moves and Market Positioning:

- Porter examines how firms can enhance their strategic positioning thr

Significance of "Competitive Strategy":

Michael E. Porter's "Competitive Strategy" has become the touchstone for managers and students of business strategy worldwide. Its frameworks, particularly the Five Forces, have become essential tools for business strategy and analysis. The book's principles provide a foundation to evaluate the competitive landscape and make informed strategic decisions.

41

"Positioning: The Battle for Your Mind" by Al Ries & Jack Trout

"Positioning: The Battle for Your Mind" is a classic in marketing literature. Written by Al Ries and Jack Trout in 1981, the book delves into the art of positioning a product, service, or even oneself in the minds of customers. This concept is crucial in the crowded marketplace where consumers are overwhelmed with information.

The Overcommunicated Society

products and brands in their minds. For a new product to be noticed, it either needs to dethrone a current leader or create a new category.

The Power of Being First:

· Ries and Trout argue that being the first in any category can give a significant advantage. The first brand or product often becomes a generic term for the entire category. For instance, many people refer to photocopying as "Xeroxing," regardless of the brand of the machine they're using.

The Fallacy of Line Extension:

· A common mistake made by companies, as observed by the authors, is over-extending their brand name into various product categories. This dilutes the brand's strength and confuses the positioning in the consumer's mind.

Positioning of a Leader:

· If you're the market leader, your strategy should be different from the rest. The leader should always position itself against the competition as a whole, not against one competitor.

Positioning of a Follower:

If you're not the leader, then your strategy should be to position yourself against the leader. This is the "against" strategy, where a brand uses the leader's strength to create a niche for itself.

Repositioning and Admitting Weakness:

- Sometimes, the best strategy is to admit a weakness, which can become a strength. Avis' "We're number two, so we try harder" campaign is a classic example of this strategy.

The Power of the Name:

- The name of a product, service, or company plays a crucial role in positioning. A wrong name can do more harm than good.

The No-Name Trap:

- Companies often use initials or abbreviations, thinking it gives them flexibility. However, such names are usually weaker in terms of positioning than full, descriptive names.

The Free-Ride Trap:

even more saturated.

Significance of "Positioning: The Battle for Your Mind":

Ries and Trout's "Positioning" introduced a revolutionary approach to marketing and advertising. Instead of focusing on the product, they shifted the focus to the mind of the prospective customer. The book underscores the importance of simplicity, clarity, and consistency in messaging. In today's digital age, with an even more cluttered marketplace, the principles of "Positioning" remain as relevant as ever.

42

"Lean Thinking" by James P. Womack & Daniel T. Jones

"Lean Thinking," published in 1996, expands upon the principles introduced in the authors' previous book, "The Machine That Changed the World." This book presents the philosophy of lean production and how organizations can apply its principles beyond manufacturing to all areas of business for improving efficiency, reducing waste, and adding value.

Defining Lean Thinking

and recognizing the steps in your business process that do not add value.

- **Value Stream:** Analyze the flow of products and services from the origin to the customer. This involves understanding every step required to design, order, and produce a product from concept to launch, order to delivery, and raw materials to the customer.
- **Flow:** Ensure that products and services flow smoothly without interruptions, delays, or bottlenecks.
- **Pull:** Production is driven by actual customer demand, not by forecasting. Products are "pulled" through the value stream.
- **Perfection:** Continuously refine processes, aiming for perfection by identifying and eliminating waste.

Waste Identification and Elimination:

- Waste is anything that doesn't add value from the customer's perspective. There are several types of waste, including overproduction, waiting, transport, extra processing, inventory, motion, and defects.

The Concept of Flow:

- Traditionally, many businesses operate in batches. Womack and Jones promote the idea of continuous flow. This method reduces waiting times, inventory levels, and defects.

Lean Transformation:

- Transforming a company to lean thinking often requires a complete overhaul of processes. This can be challenging, but the authors argue that the results in efficiency and waste reduction are worth it.

Lean Thinking in the Service Sector:

- While lean principles originated in manufacturing, especially automotive (Toyota Production System), they apply equally to the service sector. The book discusses how service industries can benefit from adopting lean thinking.

Sustainable Lean Culture:

- Implementing lean thinking isn't a one-time activity but requires building a culture of continuous improvement. It demands commitment from both top management and employees.

Case Studies and Examples:

adopted by numerous organizations around the world, leading to transformative changes in how they operate. It serves as a guide not just for businesses wanting to implement lean practices but also for anyone wanting to understand the principles that have shaped modern production and operational practices.

43

"Playing to Win: How Strategy Really Works" by A.G. Lafley & Roger L. Martin

"Playing to Win" is a strategic guide written by A.G. Lafley, the former CEO of Procter & Gamble (P&G), in collaboration with Roger L. Martin, former dean of the Rotman School of Management. Together, they outline the strategy that Lafley employed during his tenure at P&G, which resulted in the company doubling its sales, quadrupling its profits, and increasing its market value by more than $100 billion.

choices that, when addressed in a coordinated way, can lead to sustainable competitive advantage:

- **Winning Aspiration:** Define the purpose of your enterprise and what winning looks like.
- **Where to Play:** Decide where to compete, including which customers to target and in what markets or segments.
- **How to Win:** Determine how to create unique value and differentiate yourself in the chosen markets or segments.
- **Core Capabilities:** Identify what capabilities are crucial to compete and win in the chosen market.
- **Management Systems:** Create systems, measures, and structures that support your strategy.

Strategy is Iterative:

- Crafting strategy isn't linear; it requires iterating between "Where to Play" and "How to Win" until you find the optimal fit.

1. Reverse Engineering and Competitor Responses:

- Think about strategy from a competitor's perspective. By doing so, you can anticipate their moves and develop counter-strategies.

Leadership's Role in Strategy:

- Leadership should own and drive the strategy, ensuring it's a central part of the organization's discussions and decisions.

The Importance of Innovation:

- Lafley highlights that innovation was crucial for P&G's success. But he also stresses that innovation should be consistent with the strategy.

Real-world Case Studies:

- The book is peppered with real-world examples, primarily from P&G, to illustrate the principles. These examples include Olay, Tide, and Gillette, showcasing how these brands clarified their strategy to achieve market leadership.

Significance of "Playing to Win":

"Playing to Win" demystifies what strategy really is, emphasizing actionable and clear strategic choices. The book's framework is applicable across industries, making it a valuable resource for anyone looking to craft a winning strategy. Given Lafley's success at P&G, it becomes evident...

44

"Built to Last" by Jim Collins & Jerry I. Porras

"Built to Last" is a seminal business book that examines what lies behind the enduring success of some of the world's visionary companies. Instead of focusing on leadership personalities or current business trends, Collins and Porras look at the underlying factors and habits that have made certain companies stand out for decades, if not centuries. Their research spans multiple years and is based on a careful comparison between visionary companies and comparison companies in the same industry.

Visionary Companies:

- The authors define visionary companies as those that are premier institutions in their industries, are widely admired by knowledgeable peers, and have a track record of making a significant impact on the world around them.

Built to Preserve Core and Stimulate Progress:

- Visionary companies have a core ideology that remains constant, while their specific business strategies and practices endlessly adapt to a changing world. This dual capability allows them to be consistent yet adaptable.

Clock Building, Not Time Telling:

- Visionary companies focus on building institutions that endure over time, rather than emphasizing a particular market or product success. It's akin to building a clock that keeps accurate time over the long term rather than just telling the time once.

Embrace the Genius of the 'And':

- Rather than being oppressed by the "Tyranny of the 'Or'", visionary companies embrace both extremes on a number of dimensions at the same time. For instance, they focus on being consistent and adaptable, being cautious and bold, etc.

core ideology.

Try a Lot of Stuff and Keep What Works:

· Through experimentation and trial and error, these companies innovate and evolve. They're more evolutionary than
revolutionary, advancing through incremental progress.

Homegrown Management:

· Visionary companies tend to promote insiders who understand and exemplify the company's core values.

Big Hairy Audacious Goals (BHAGs):

· These companies use ambitious goals to progress forward,
ensuring they remain at the forefront of their industries.

Preserve the Core/Stimulate Progress:

· The essence of a visionary company comes in the balance
of preserving core values and ideologies while being open
to change and progress in all other areas.

Significance of "Built to Last":

"Built to Last" offers readers a deep dive into the foundational
elements of companies that have stood the test of time. The
insights aren't just historical recounts but actionable lessons
for leaders and managers striving to build enduring compa-

nies. The distinction between core values (which should be preserved) and business practices (which should evolve) is especially crucial in today's rapidly changing business environment.

45

"Traction" by Gino Wickman

In "Traction," Gino Wickman introduces the Entrepreneurial Operating System (EOS)®, a practical method for helping business leaders and entrepreneurs achieve clarity, discipline, and accountability. Through this system, businesses can align their teams and execute their vision. The EOS is based on the idea that every business faces similar frustrations, including growth ceilings, lack of control, and people issues. Wickman breaks down the process of implementing the EOS into six key components:

Vision:

- Everyone in the organization needs to be on the same page regarding where the company is headed and how it will get there. This clarity ensures that all efforts and resources are aligned with achieving the business's overarching objectives.

People:

- The right people need to be in the right seats. This means that team members not only share the company's core values but also excel in their specific roles. Wickman provides tools to help assess and position employees effectively.

Data:

- To get a clear pulse on the organization, you need a high-level scorecard. By focusing on a handful of critical numbers, leaders can get an instantaneous snapshot of the company's health and its progress towards achieving its goals.

Issues:

- Every organization faces obstacles. The EOS provides a systematic process for recognizing, prioritizing, and resolving these issues before they escalate, ensuring they don't hinder growth or operations.

Process:

now gain traction. This involves instilling discipline and accountability throughout the organization, ensuring that everyone executes the company's vision consistently and effectively.

In addition to these six components, Wickman also introduces practical tools and disciplines, including:

- The **Traction Meeting Pulse™**, which keeps teams aligned and focused.
- **Rocks**, or quarterly priorities, to ensure continuous progress.
- The **Issue Solving Track™**, a structured approach to addressing and resolving challenges.

Significance of "Traction":

"Traction" provides a blueprint for entrepreneurs and leaders to systematically grow and manage their businesses. Instead of relying on quick fixes or chasing the latest management fads, the EOS offers a timeless, holistic approach to business operations. It's especially beneficial for small to medium-sized businesses that may lack formal structures, helping them gain control, align their teams, and achieve consistent results.

46

"Emotional Intelligence" by Daniel Goleman

In "Emotional Intelligence," Daniel Goleman introduces the concept of emotional intelligence (EI) and makes a compelling argument for its critical role in personal and professional success. He suggests that while traditional cognitive intelligence (or IQ) is important, EI can be an even more potent indicator of success in life.

Self-Regulation:

- This component refers to managing, controlling, and redirecting disruptive emotions and impulses. It's the ability to think before acting, manage emotional reactions to all situations and people, and adapt to changing circumstances.

Motivation:

- Goleman identifies a type of motivation driven by an underlying passion for the work itself rather than external factors like money or status. This intrinsic motivation is a powerful force that drives individuals to be productive and effective in their professions.

Empathy:

- Empathy is the ability to understand the emotions of others and to treat people according to their emotional reactions. It involves recognizing the emotional needs of others and considering those needs in one's interactions and decisions.

Social Skills:

- This component encompasses skills such as effective communication, conflict management, collaboration, and leadership. People with strong social skills can build rapport and maintain healthy, productive relationships.

Key Insights:

- **Brain Science:** Goleman delves into the neuroscience behind emotions, describing how the brain processes feelings and reacts to emotional stimuli.
- **The "Amygdala Hijack":** One of the book's well-known concepts is the "amygdala hijack," where the amygdala (a part of the brain associated with emotions) overtakes rational thinking in moments of intense emotion, like anger or fear.
- **The Cost of Emotional Illiteracy:** Goleman points out the societal and personal costs of lacking emotional intelligence, from impulsive acts and violence to mental health challenges.
- **Improving EI:** Emotional intelligence is not static. Goleman posits that with appropriate training and practice, individuals can enhance their EI, benefiting both personal and professional aspects of their lives.

Significance of "Emotional Intelligence":

When "Emotional Intelligence"

profound implications for education, organizational leadership, and interpersonal relationships.

47

"Awaken the Giant Within" by Tony Robbins

"Awaken the Giant Within" is a comprehensive self-help guide where Tony Robbins shares strategies and techniques for mastering emotions, finances, relationships, and life. Drawing upon his experiences as a life coach and his personal journey, Robbins offers insights, tools, and structures for individuals to take charge of their lives.

Mastering Emotions:

- The book delves into the nature of emotions, how they influence behavior, and strategies for gaining control over them. Robbins provides a 'Vocabulary of Emotions' to better categorize feelings and offers techniques to transition from disempowering emotions to empowering ones.

Life Control Through Questions:

- Robbins introduces the idea that the quality of one's life is determined by the quality of questions they ask themselves. By shifting from limiting questions to empowering ones, individuals can drive positive change in their lives.

Belief Systems:

- Our beliefs shape our actions and destiny. Robbins discusses the power of belief systems and how one can adopt empowering beliefs while discarding limiting ones.

The Power of Visualization:

- Robbins emphasizes the significance of mental conditioning. He suggests techniques for creating a compelling future through visualization, setting the stage for actualizing those visions.

Neuro-Associative Conditioning (NAC):

- Robbins presents his version of behavior modification –

NAC. He argues that by associating pain with undesirable behaviors and pleasure with desirable actions, one can create lasting behavioral change.

Financial Mastery:

- Moving beyond the psychological aspects, Robbins offers guidance on managing, investing, and growing personal wealth, emphasizing the importance of intelligent financial practices for overall life satisfaction.

Relationship Mastery:

- Robbins explores the dynamics of relationships and how understanding personal and partner needs can lead to more fulfilling connections. He also introduces 'The Six Human Needs' – certainty, variety, significance, connection/love, growth, and contribution – as a framework for understanding human behavior.

The book stands as a testament to Robbins' prowess as a life coach, motivational speaker, and author, providing readers with tools and frameworks to instigate profound change in their lives.

48

"Never Split the Difference" by Chris Voss

"Never Split the Difference" is a guide to negotiation, authored by Chris Voss, a former lead international kidnapping negotiator for the FBI. Voss brings his high-stakes experiences to the realm of business negotiation and everyday interactions, offering techniques that can be applied in various situations. The title "Never Split the Difference" underscores his main idea: in critical negotiations, especially ones involving human lives, splitting the d way for a constructive dialogue.

Tactical Empathy:

· This concept revolves around understanding the feelings and mindset of another in the moment and also hearing what is behind those feelings. It's about validating the emotions without necessarily agreeing with them.

Mirror Technique:

· Mirroring involves repeating the last few words spoken by the counterpart. This technique encourages the other party to elaborate more, often revealing additional information.

Label Their Fears:

· By vocalizing and addressing the other party's fears, you can diffuse potential roadblocks in the negotiation.

Establish a "That's Right" Moment:

· The goal is to get the counterpart to say "that's right" in acknowledgment that you've understood their point of view. This builds rapport and paves the way for agreement.

Beware of "Yes" – Aim for "No":

· A "yes" can be deceptive and might be a counterfeit agreement. Instead, aim to get a "no" which can give clarity on the counterpart's position and provide a genuine platform to proceed.

Create the Illusion of Control:

- Ask calibrated, open-ended questions to let the other side feel like they are in control.

Use the "Ackerman Model":

- A step-by-step negotiation strategy where you start with an extreme initial offer and use calculated increments to reach the desired amount, all while using the other techniques to extract information and build rapport.

Determine Your BATNA (Best Alternative To a Negotiated Agreement):

- Know what alternatives you have if the negotiation fails. This not only provides clarity but also strengthens your negotiating position.

Voss's approach challenges conventional negotiation wisdom. Instead of promoting compromise and logic, he underscores the significance of emotion and human connection. The techniques are not about "winning" the negotiation but about building understanding and rapport to achieve desirable outcomes.

"Never Split the Difference" goes beyond business transactions and deal-making. Its principles are applicable in various aspects of daily life, whether it's buying a car, negotiating a salary, or even resolving personal disputes. Voss provides readers with actionable tactics derived from the real-world stakes of hostage negotiation, making the book a unique and invaluable resource on the art of negotiation.

49

"The 4-Hour Workweek" by Timothy Ferriss

"The 4-Hour Workweek" by Timothy Ferriss is a guide that challenges the conventional wisdom of working long hours in a traditional job to earn a living and then retiring late in life. Instead, Ferriss proposes a radical new approach to lifestyle design, emphasizing the idea of achieving more with less time through automation, outsourcing, and focusing on what's truly important.

engage in other desired activities.

DEAL Formula:

- Ferriss presents a four-step process, encapsulated by the acronym DEAL:
- **D for Definition:** Redefine success. Rather than adhering to societal norms of success, define what you truly want.
- **E for Elimination:** Focus on the essential. Apply the 80/20 rule, suggesting that 80% of results come from 20% of efforts. Eliminate or delegate unnecessary tasks.
- **A for Automation:** Create automated income streams. Use the concept of "muses," which are businesses or investments that require minimal ongoing effort.
- **L for Liberation:** Achieve the freedom to live and work from anywhere.

Selective Ignorance:

- It's not about being informed but about being selectively informed. Avoid unnecessary information and news, focusing only on what is relevant and actionable.

Outsourcing Life:

- Use virtual assistants or other services to handle tasks that don't require your personal touch, allowing you to focus on higher-value activities.

Mini Retirements:

- Instead of deferring life dreams to a distant retirement, take "mini-retirements" throughout life. Travel, learn new skills, or explore passions without waiting for the traditional retirement age.

Overcoming Fear:

- Ferriss discusses the concept of "fear-setting" as opposed to "goal-setting." By visualizing the worst-case scenarios and then devising strategies to mitigate them, you can act despite fears.

End of Time Management:

- Prioritize tasks based on importance and outcome, not on the time they take. It's about results, not hours.

Creating a Product-Based Business:

- Ferriss emphasizes the value of creating businesses based on produc..

adventure, and fulfillment.

However, it's essential to understand that the title "4-Hour Workweek" is more of a symbol of efficiency and liberation than a literal recommendation. The book's real value lies in its broader message: challenging societal norms, thinking big, and questioning the status quo to live life on one's terms.

50

"The Everything Store: Jeff Bezos and the Age of Amazon" by Brad Stone

"The Everything Store" by Brad Stone delves into the history of Amazon and the life of its enigmatic founder, Jeff Bezos. Using a wide range of sources, including interviews with current and former Amazon employees, Stone charts the company's rise from an online bookstore to the colossal e-commerce platform it is today.

- Bezos's philosophy is built around the customer. Innovations like user reviews, even negative ones about products, reflected this ethos. Bezos believed that focusing on the customer would ensure long-term profitability.

Expansion and Diversification:

- Amazon expanded its product categories and ventured into selling music, videos, and electronics. Later, they would grow into cloud computing with AWS, e-readers with Kindle, and even entertainment with Amazon Studios.

Internal Culture:

- Stone delves into Amazon's intense corporate culture with its notorious hardworking ethos, often characterized by Bezos's demanding standards and the company's leadership principles.

Competition and Confrontation:

- Amazon's journey was not without challenges. The company had showdowns with competitors, publishers, and even its workforce. Stone recounts confrontations with companies like Barnes & Noble and Diapers.com, detailing Amazon's aggressive tactics.

Innovation and Failure:

- Not all of Amazon's ventures were successful. The company saw failures like the Fire Phone. However, Bezos's willingness to take risks and learn from failures was an integral part of the company's DNA.

Bezos's Vision:

- Beyond just e-commerce, Stone highlights Bezos's broader vision, evident in acquisitions like The Washington Post and the founding of the space company Blue Origin.

Significance of "The Everything Store":

Brad Stone's "The Everything Store" offers a rare, comprehensive insight into one of the most transformative companies of our time. The book paints a portrait of a visionary and, at times, ruthless leader in Jeff Bezos, whose relentless drive has been a significant factor in Amazon's success.

The narrative does not shy away from controversies and criticisms, offering a balanced view of both Amazon's commendable innovations and its points of contention in the business world.

51

"Tools of Titans" by Tim Ferriss

"Tools of Titans" is a compilation of lessons and insights Tim Ferriss gathered from interviewing more than 200 world-class performers on his podcast, "The Tim Ferriss Show". The book is structured in three main sections, reflecting Ben Franklin's famous quote: "Early to bed and early to rise, makes a man healthy, wealthy, and wise."

Healthy:

- In this section, Ferriss explores the habits, routines, and strategies the Titans use to maintain their physical and mental health. Topics range from exercise routines, sleep habits, meditation techniques, and even dietary practices

- **Key Insights:**
- Many successful individuals prioritize meditation or mindfulness practices.
- The importance of a regular sleep schedule and optimal sleep environment.

- The benefits of various types of diets and fasting protocols.

Wealthy:

- This portion dives into the practices and principles that the interviewed subjects attribute to their financial and career success.

- **Key Insights:**
- The value of creating automated income streams.
- The importance of negotiation skills.
- Approaches to investing, both in terms of money and time.
- Lessons on entrepreneurship, including the significance of taking calculated risks.

Wise:

- Ferriss delves into the philosophical, spiritual, and intellectual frameworks that guide the lives of the Titans.

- Key Insights:

Notable Figures Featured: The book showcases a diverse range of individuals, from tech moguls like Peter Thiel and Marc Andreessen to creatives like Maria Popova and Malcolm Gladwell, and from athletes like Arnold Schwarzenegger to meditation experts like Sam Harris.

Significance of "Tools of Titans":

"Tools of Titans" offers readers a unique opportunity to peek into the lives and minds of some of the most successful and accomplished individuals across various fields. Its format, broken down into bite-sized yet profound insights, makes it a valuable reference that one can revisit multiple times. The book underscores that while there's no single path to success, certain habits, mindsets, and strategies are recurrent among those who achieve greatness.

52

Closing Thoughts

The journey we've embarked on together has covered a vast landscape of ideas, strategies, and insights from some of the most brilliant minds in the world of business. From leadership to strategy, from innovation to communication, and from personal development to industry-specific insights, we've delved deep into the collective knowledge amassed over decades.

Key Takeaways:

1. Lifelong Learning:

The world of business is constantly evolving, and staying still means getting left behind. To stay relevant and ahead of the curve, continuous learning is paramount.

2. The Power of Perspective:

Each author brought their unique viewpoint. Recognize the value in seeking diverse perspectives, as this broadens understanding and facilitates better decision-making.

3. Resilience and Adaptability:

Many books highlighted the importance of resilience in the face of challenges and the ability to adapt to change. This isn't just about surviving but thriving amid uncertainty.

4. The Human Element:

Whether it's understanding consumer behavior, leading a team, or managing oneself, the human element is central to business. Emotional intelligence, empathy, and effective communication stand out as key pillars of success.

5. Ethics and Integrity:

Success without integrity is hollow. Many authors underscored the importance of doing business ethically and creating value not just for shareholders but for society at large.

Your own learning journey

You might ask, "What next? How do I apply all this knowledge?" Start by recognizing that this book isn't a definitive manual but rather a starting point. Business, at its heart, isn't just about facts and figures—it's about people, relationships, and the pursuit of meaningful objectives.

Here's a suggested roadmap:

- **Personalize Your Knowledge:** Understand that not all advice will apply uniformly. Reflect on each book's insights and tailor them to your unique situation.
- **Act Incrementally:** Instead of trying to implement everything simultaneously, choose a few key insights that resonate and start there.
- **Engage in Dialogue:** Share your learnings with colleagues, mentors, or peers. Engage in discussions, debates, and brainstorming sessions.
- **Revisit and Refresh:** Knowledge is like

May your endeavours be purposeful, and may the wisdom from these pages empower you to reach unprecedented heights. Here's to the business leaders of tomorrow, inspired by the giants of yesterday and today.

Printed in Great Britain
by Amazon

29212191R00106